Praise for The Global Brain

"One of those rare books that send a tingle down the spine."
New Internationalist, U.K.

"The most exciting and significant book I have ever read."
Bernard Benson, author, *The Peace Book*

"Peter Russell has laid forth the evolutionary blueprint for the future. *The Global Brain* comes just in the nick of time."
Barbara Marx Hubbard, author, *The Revelation*

"It ranks with the best of Fritjof Capra and Lyall Watson as part of a trend in communicating ideas about mankind's inner self and our relation to the physical world; it is very well written, and it deserves to be a best seller."
John Gribbin, *New Scientist*

"I was more impressed with your book than I have been with any that I have read recently. It establishes a rational, scientific basis for the more intuitive, spiritual channelings."
Ken Carey, author, *The Starseed Transmissions*

"*The Global Brain* certainly has helped advance our thinking about the earth being alive."
Jim Swan, Project Director, U.S. National Audubon Society

"Through this evolutionary odyssey I experience the thrill of mind meeting Mind."
Ram Dass, author, *Be There Now*

"A clear and exciting survey of some of the most important ideas in the world at the moment."
Colin Wilson, author, *The Outside*

"Peter Russell's suggestion of an evolutionary leap into greater spiritual awareness is the only possible route forward for mankind."

Prof. John Taylor, King's College, London

"Your discussion of what have been difficult subjects for me is so economical and clear that I feel as though a burden has been lifted."

Carl Flygt, U.S.A.

"I picked up this book expecting to scoff all the way to the last page and ended up with a tremendous sense of optimism for the human race. The book as a whole has had a positive effect on my view of the future of mankind. I hope it does the same for all other readers."

Catholic Herald, U.K.

"To a world badly in need of new visions and realistic optimism, Peter Russell offers a bold hypothesis . . . . His thesis is bound to be the subject of much discussion in the trying years ahead."

Willis Harman, President, Institute of Noetic Sciences

"In my view, it's one of the most important books so far this century."

Peter Lemesurier, author, *Beyond All Belief*

"At about one o'clock I got up, closed the window, propped myself up in bed and opened *The Global Brain*. At 5 o'clock I closed the book, having made a remarkable journey in your company. The book is truly a colossal accomplishment."

Frances Horn, U.S.A.

"I am thrilled at the attempt to think on this holistic scale. Peter Russell brings together scientific knowledge and the holistic vision of the spiritual nature of the Universe and Man."

Sir George Trevelyan, U.K.

"From your writing I sense a genuine respect for the human proposition as well as the mark of actual personal development done and not theoretical intellectualism."

A.M. Corper, *Holland*

"Peter Russell's thoughtful analyses will help to bring about an urgently needed transformation of attitudes."

Prof. Brian Josephson, Nobel Laureate, U.K.

"So far, I am afraid, such ideas are mostly hidden in voluminous and difficult to read books for insiders. Your book is really a rare exception."

Gerhard Breidenstein, Germany

"It is unusual to find so profound a book so lucidly written; its subject is 'in the air' and Peter Russell has magnificently crystalized and developed it. I believe he will open new doors to many people's perceptions. I read the book almost at a sitting, in great excitement."

Brian Aldiss, author, *The Long Afternoon of Earth*

"Through fifty years in the Christian ministry, and the reading of endless books, I have not read anything so comprehensive, and so lucidly written on the basic origins and meaning of our earthly existence.

It is the sort of book that if I had the money I would pay for copies to be generally distributed . . . ."

Rev. Charles W. Harrington, U.K.

"I think this is the most important book since the Bible. I want to order a hundred and send them to my friends, and suggest that they do the same."

Anne Seggerman, U.S.A.

"A timely reminder that, for the first time in evolution, there is a species which has control not only of its own destiny but that of every other living thing on this planet."

Lyall Watson, author, *Supernature*

"You will be glad—or amazed—to know that I bought 12 copies of *The Global Brain*. . .. It is the only book for years and years that I have gone straight back to page one to read all over again, the very moment I finished the last page."

Sarah Woodhouse, Lancing College, U.K.

"I just can't describe the feeling I have, when reading your book. Thank you for this beautiful personal experience. You've done humankind a great service. What do you do for an encore after something like this?"

Jeff Strong, U.S.A.

"I stole your book from (a mutual friend) and loved it. I'd ordered 4 for my children. It is now to become 44 as we have to substitute them for the Gideon Bibles in some houses we are building."

Charles Nuttall, Bahamas

"Very inspiring. Already I have five more copies that I intend to give to some close friends at Christmas and will ask them, if they enjoyed it as much as I did, to do the same. It could become the first ever literary chain letter!"

Brian Irons, U.K.

"I read your marvellous book *The Global Brain* some years ago and have since recommended it to many others. I hope that it has been the success I feel it ought to be. Needs to be, even, if we are to move on to a saner world."

Salamah Pope, Indonesia

"It is the spirit I like most in your books! The optimism! That we really need today. Then the vision! That we also need badly! Then the extensive research you have made so the questions get illuminated from all possible angles! Rarely I can say so much positive about a book."

Tomas Almberg, Denmark

THE GLOBAL
BRAIN AWAKENS

Our Next Evolutionary Leap

Also by Peter Russell:

The TM Technique
The Brain Book
The Upanishads
Passing Thoughts
The Creative Manager
The White Hole in Time

THE GLOBAL BRAIN AWAKENS
Our Next Evolutionary Leap

PETER RUSSELL

GLOBAL BRAIN INC.
PALO ALTO, CA, U.S.A.

Library of Congress Cataloging in Publication Data

Russell, Peter, 1946-
   The global brain awakens : our next evolutionary leap / Peter
Russell. -- 2d ed.
   p. cm.
   Rev. ed. of: The global brain, 1983.
   Includes bibliographical references and index.
   ISBN: 1-885261-05-5.

   1. Biology -- Philosophy.   2. Gaia hypothesis.   3. Biosphere
4. Evolution. 5. Consciousness. I. Russell, Peter, 1946- The global brain.
II. Title.
QH331.R78 1995   574.01
                                        QBI94-2609
ISBN 1-885261-05-05
(1st Edition ISBN 087477-248-6Pa)

Requests for such permission should be addressed to:
Global Brain Inc.
555 Bryant Street, #210
Palo Alto, California, 94301-1704, U.S.A.
Tel. 1-800-U-GO-GLOBAL

1st Edition published by J.P. Tarcher, Inc., as *The Global Brain* (1983)
1st Edition edited by Stephanie E. Bernstein
2nd Edition edited by Gloria St. John, Danielle LaPorte, Orion Kopelman

Printed by McNaughton & Gunn, Saline, Michigan
Cover design by Lightbourne Images, Ashland, Oregon
Layout design by Nora A. Hooper, Sarasota, Florida
Typeset in Berkeley Oldstyle 12 point on 16
Author's photograph by Alexandra Gründell

Global Brain Inc.'s mission is to accelerate the development of appropriate
technological products and personal evolution through consciousness-
raising publications and consulting services; for the purposes of furthering
the formation of the Global Brain.

CONTENTS

PART ONE

THE BIGGER PICTURE

PART TWO

EVOLUTION PAST, PRESENT, AND FUTURE

PART THREE

INNER EVOLUTION

EPILOGUE

FOREWORD

When Peter Russell's book, *The Global Brain*, was first published in 1982, it was well ahead of its time. Its strongest appeal was to futurists of all kinds—business people, social critics, and others who are insatiably curious about the day after tomorrow.

During the intervening years the notion of a global brain has become almost a given, at least insofar as the world-wide communications link. Events like the "Live Aid" concert and dramatic international cooperation, as in the rescue of the whales in the Bering Strait, pointed out the power of our communications network and the connect-edness of all peoples.

But we are a little slower in recognizing the extent to which we are linked spiritually and psychologically. Many of the corporate clients who call on Peter Russell as a consultant or teacher are probably unaware of his earlier works: *The TM Technique*, *The Brain Book*, and a translation of *The Upanishads*. Russell came to his vision of an emerging world-mind through reflection and personal insights over many years.

I first met the author in 1978, shortly after I had begun to publish *Brain/Mind Bulletin*, a Los Angeles-based newsletter devoted to cutting-edge research. While visiting London I met with several subscribers. My visit with Peter at a sidewalk café was the beginning of a long, immensely educational and entertaining friendship.

The trait I most value about him is the way his work regularly changes direction to reflect his new insights and understandings. He does not repeat himself. He has not tried to spin a single idea, however good, into fabric enough to clothe an entire career. Rather he observes, reflects, and records his reactions in a helpful, direct way.

Is there a global brain?

Research in recent years suggests that human beings are capable of subtle communication. For example, when experimenters in Mexico instructed two people, who were sitting silently in a lead-lined enclosure, to tune into each other, their brainwave patterns suddenly became synchronized. Female friends who live in the same dormitory hall tend to become synchronized in their menstrual rhythms. Men develop temperature cycles that match the ovarian cycles of the women with whom they live.

Bonds between infants and mothers, mysterious modes of communication among animals and insects, and individual incidents of apparent rapport—all these are clues that something ties all of life together. Judging from surveys, the majority of people have experienced inexplicable communications from others in distant places.

No doubt such links seem mysterious only because we

have too primitive an understanding of nature's complex energies. In the earlier stages of our physics we expected to identify concrete building blocks of matter, but matter disappeared into elusive subatomic particles that behave more like thoughts than things. In our medical hypotheses we imagined clear-cut boundaries between the tangible physical world and the invisible realm of thought. Now the new scientific field of psychoneuroimmunology is identifying mechanisms whereby our emotions directly affect our health.

At the same time, the "Gaia Hypothesis" is attracting ever more serious, as well as popular, interest. The idea, introduced by James Lovelock, that Earth is a living entity, with potential for self-healing and self-maintenance, seems increasingly plausible. But Lovelock also acknowledges, now, that humanity might tip the balance so seriously that Earth cannot recover—at least, not in time for our continued well-being. In other words, our planet might survive our escapades, but our species might perish.

What difference does it make to you and me if we are the cells of a global brain rather than isolated inhabitants of a planet? For one thing, the fine line dividing "individual" and "social" becomes more a convention than a reality.

Peter Russell points out the urgent need to ensure that our global brain is sane rather then insane. Each of us "neurons" can take a few steps toward collective sanity. We can make sure, for example, to conserve physical resources in our personal lives. We can discover new methods for personal renewal. We can try to elect and support leaders who seem to respect the interdependence of all people. We can *be* those leaders.

We can also move beyond survival. We can deepen our own sense of meaning by using our imaginations. We can see ourselves as part of a greater whole, a humanity emerging into the springtime of a new understanding.

Marilyn Ferguson

Preface to the Second Edition

I wrote the first edition of *The Global Brain* during the late 1970s and early 1980s, and much has happened in the following decade. Technology has leapt ahead at an unprecedented rate — especially in the fields of information processing and telecommunications. Terms like "Internet" and "information superhighway", which are common parlance today, were virtually unheard of ten years ago, and so were faxes, modems, and laptop computers. Looking back over the original version of the book, I was relieved to find that my predictions in this area had in general been born out, but the data on which I had based these predictions was clearly out-of-date. For this reason alone a new edition was called for.

As well as being about our burgeoning global information network, *The Global Brain Awakens* is also about social and personal change, and much has changed in these areas as well. We have seen the fall of the Berlin Wall and the end of Soviet-style communism, triggering major political and commercial realignments. Over the same period there has been a growing realization of the very real threat we are posing to our own environment, and an awakening to the fact that we are one people, living on one planet, with one common destiny. In these areas also the book needed updating.

THE GLOBAL NERVOUS SYSTEM GROWS

One personally memorable symbol of increasing planetary awareness was the Live Aid Concert in 1985. Spurred by the horror of hunger and destitution among fellow beings, a billion people around the world simultaneously watched a concert taking place across the planet. Halfway through, a fly walked across my television screen. As I watched the fly I thought how it was probably aware only of the patch of color beneath its feet. It had no idea of the picture that was created from the million dots upon my screen. Then I realized that I was but a fly on the screen of a planetary broadcast, aware only of myself and the image in front of me. Who knows what picture was being generated across the billion other minds that were tuned in to the same input?

Television has brought the world closer in other ways. Portable video cameras in Karachi can transmit events to satellites 22,000 miles above the equator, which relay them to television studios around the Earth, where they are edited, processed and broadcast "live" to the rest of the world. The eye of the portable video camera has become an eye of the "global brain".

This capacity for instant social feedback has played a significant role in accelerating the pace of change. The Romanian revolution in December 1989, which seemed to rush itself through in time for the new decade, was very much a revolution by television. The leaders of the revolution had a direct channel of communication to the people, who in turn could watch the news as they made it. Without this instant feedback, the revolution may have taken a great deal longer, or never have happened at all.

Nowhere is our accelerating pace of change reflected more clearly than in the increasing amounts of broadcast time dedicated to change itself—i.e., the "news". Twenty years ago we had fifteen-minute bulletins, perhaps twice an evening. In the 1980s we became accustomed to one-hour news programs on every channel—and at breakfast and lunchtime, as well as in the evenings. "News," claimed BBC chairman Marmaduke Hussey recently, "is our fastest expanding area of programming." In the U.S.A., entire TV channels are devoted to the news. Ted Turner, the undisputed leader of this trend, has established his 24-hour news station, CNN, on five satellites spanning the globe. Now anyone, anywhere, can tune into the news at any time— and other media barons are in hot pursuit.

Satellite television has not been the only factor behind our increasing globalization. Mobile telephones, fax machines, and computer networks, all fledgling technologies ten years ago, are now household items for many, giving us instant access to each other, wherever we might be. This increasing ease of communication has had its own impact on world events. In the Tiananmen Square uprising in China in the spring of 1989, students used college fax ma-

chines to communicate with each other and send information to colleagues around the world, who in turn faxed back
their own reports. Authoritarian control of the news had
become a much harder task.

The nerve fibers of the global network have also continued to develop rapidly. The world now has over 900
million telephones: about 17 for every 100 people on Earth.
They may not be evenly distributed—Sweden has 64 per
100 people, the U.S.A. has 51 per 100, Europe 22, South
America six, and Africa and China only one per 100—yet
in every country the number is growing steadily. By the
time you read this it will probably have reached a billion.

PLANETARY AWARENESS

The 1980s were also the years in which the environment
hit the headlines. For two decades a small but growing
band of people had been voicing their concern about the
damage humankind was causing to its surroundings, and
the potential disasters that lay ahead. Yet frequently they
were dismissed as "unduly alarmist"— or else simply ignored. As far as the media was concerned, the environment
was a minority interest.

But in the summer of 1988 global alarm bells rang loud
and clear. The news was now full of stories of dolphins
dying by the thousands, lethal waste washing up on beaches,
holes in the ozone layer, global warming, crop failures, poi-
soned lakes, dying trees, and burning forests. The global
mind had become conscious of its body.

Now, as we move through the final decade of this millennium, it is rapidly becoming clear that environmental issues can no longer be ignored. They pose the most serious threat humanity has ever experienced, and, if not given our full attention, may possibly nullify any plans we have for a party on New Millennium's Eve.

More significantly, it is not only individuals who are beginning to awaken to the urgency. There is a realization that business must move from the profit-oriented goal of economic growth to the ethic of sustainable development, in which "environmental capital" such as soil, forest, and ground and surface waters are given the same importance as financial capital. A growing number of corporate leaders recognize that if there is going to be a world in which business can continue to operate, it needs to be mindful of its own ecology. It should begin to regard itself and the environment as a single system, a closed loop in which everything is ultimately recycled. From this perspective, the value of an enterprise is measured not only in financial terms, but also in terms of whether or not it leaves the Earth in as good a state as it found her.

THE CONSCIOUSNESS CRISIS

Valuable as sustainable economic models may be in reducing ecological damage, they will not on their own be sufficient to meet the challenges ahead. The changes we need to make go far deeper. In order to develop a caring attitude towards the world, we need to develop a new model of ourselves, a new sense of who we are and what it is we really want. We have to move beyond the limited perception that sees fulfillment only in the joys we can derive from the world around. We must come to value our inner development as much as, if not more than, our material development. In other words, we need a change of attitude, a change of heart.

Recently some political leaders have been extolling the value of such a change in consciousness. For example, Vaclav Havel, former President of Czechoslovakia, speaking to a joint meeting of the U.S. Senate and Congress in February 1990, said that twenty-one years of suppression had given him one certainty:

> Consciousness precedes being, and not the other way around, as the Marxists claim. For this reason, the salvation of this human world lies nowhere else than in the human heart, in the human power to reflect, in human meekness, and in human responsibility.

He concluded by arguing:

> Without a global revolution in the sphere of human consciousness, nothing will change for the better in the sphere of our being as humans, and the catastrophe towards which this world is headed— the ecological, social demographic or general breakdown of civilization—will be unavoidable.

Perhaps the most important question humanity has to ask itself is whether this trend towards inner awakening is occurring fast enough. The values that dominate are, by and large, those that come from the need to sustain and defend our egocentric sense of identity. We know, for instance, that motor vehicle exhaust is a major contributor to the greenhouse effect, the repercussions of which seriously threaten the future of human civilization. Yet few people are willing to forego the luxury of a car—indeed, automobile sales are still on the increase.

It is clear that the destruction of the ozone layer poses an even greater threat—not only to us, but to all life on Earth. Although we may be curtailing the production of chlorofluorocarbons (CFCs), other equally dangerous substances are still being produced, used and dispersed into the atmosphere, on the grounds that "no satisfactory replacement is yet on the market." Meanwhile governments are reluctant to impose tighter pollution controls on industry for fear that they may lose their support, and thus their power. Humanity would seem to be caught in a conflict between its self-created needs for security, approval, and power, and the need to behave in ways which are life-enhancing and in harmony with the environment.

Much of the blame for this self-centered attitude has been put upon our love for money. But this is not the root of the problem; it is only a symptom of a deeper issue. Our true bottom line is our own inner well-being. Behind everything that we do is the belief that it will lead, in one way or another, to greater satisfaction, fulfillment, happiness, or peace of mind.

There is nothing wrong with seeking happiness or peace of mind. It is the natural motivation behind all our thoughts and actions. Where we have gone wrong is in assuming that whether or not we are at peace depends upon what is happening in the world around us. This is why we value money. It gives us the power to change our experience. It buys us security, recognition, stimulus, or whatever else we think we need. And we believe that if we had these needs fulfilled, then we ourselves would be fulfilled. Yet, all too often, we find our salvation to be temporary. Soon these needs arise again, and we are driven to exploit the world once more in our pursuit of inner peace.

This attachment to the material world as our primary source of happiness lies at the root of much of the craziness that humanity perpetrates upon the world. It is this that leads us to consume resources we do not need, to treat other people as elements in an equation, to discharge our refuse out of sight, and to mistreat and abuse our own bodies.

Yet our culture continues to tell us that this attachment is not only normal but correct. Much of our education focuses on knowing the ways of the world in order that we may better use it for our own ends. The daily deluge of television, radio, newspapers, magazines, and billboards reinforces the belief that happiness comes from what we do or have. Wherever we turn we seem to find confirmation that outer well-being determines inner well-being. We have, in effect, been hypnotized into accepting that this external side of the equation is all there is. As Ralph Waldo Emerson wrote more than 100 years ago in his essay *Self-Reliance:*

> Society everywhere is in conspiracy against the manhood of every one of its members. Society is a joint-stock company in which the members agree, for the better securing of his bread to each shareholder, to surrender the liberty and culture of the eater.

THE CHALLENGE AHEAD

If we are to stop abusing our world we need to let go of our attachments. This does not, as people often suppose, mean *detachment*, which implies complacency and not caring, and for some, going without material well-being and comforts. It is, quite simply, *non-attachment*. Material well-being and comforts are valued for what they are, but they are not seen as the sole or primary source of our inner well-being. In a state of non-attachment we no longer believe that what we have or do will provide the peace that we each seek. As a result we are free to care more fully for other people, and for all living beings.

Thus the most important fight of all at this crucial stage in our evolution is not the fight against hunger, the fight against inflation, the fight against pollution, or the fight against corrupt governments. Each is very necessary and cannot be relaxed. However, they will not be won until we have also won the fight within ourselves: the struggle between our self-centered mode of thinking and the inner knowing that there is more to life than gratifying our ego-centric needs.

The basic wisdom already exists. It is there in the spiritual traditions of all cultures; it has been articulated by the saints and wise people of all times; it is there inside every one of us. It is the truth we each know deep within. The question is how do we tap this wisdom? Can we live it, rather than just talk about it? Can it permeate our minds and hearts, enabling us to put this wisdom into practice? This is the real challenge facing us as we move into the next millennium.

An Optimistic Outlook?

Over the years many people have approached me to say how refreshing they find my optimism. I find this surprising. I do not consider myself an optimist in the sense that I believe everything will work out fine. Nor am I a pessimist. I do believe that we are passing through the most exciting, the most challenging, and the most dangerous times that humanity has ever experienced. Indeed, they may well be the most challenging times the planet herself has ever experienced. And the outcome is far from certain. If humanity does not wise up rapidly, then it seems very likely that this current phase of human civilization will come to a sad and perhaps painful end.

There are those who believe it may already be too late. We may already have caused irreversible damage to the environment, and it is only a matter of time before we suffer the tragic consequences. Some argue that the inertia of political systems is so great that, even if it were possible to avert disaster, the appropriate changes will not be made in time.

While there clearly are grounds for such pessimism, we should not forget that the totally unexpected can change all our forecasts. Almost no one foresaw the dramatic turn of affairs in eastern Europe during the latter months of 1989. Those who did see the possibility of such changes expected them five to fifteen years in the future. Even now, no one knows to where they will lead. The world may become more stable as a result, or it may be thrown into even greater turmoil. Only time will tell.

We have entered the age not of prophecy and prediction, but of the unexpected. Ahead of us may lie many more unexpected political changes, unexpected economic changes, unexpected disasters, unexpected changes in climate, unexpected changes in thinking, unexpected discoveries, unexpected changes of heart among our leaders—and possibly changes so unexpected that we cannot even imagine what they might be. Moreover, as the pace of change continues to increase, the unexpected will come upon us faster and faster.

There are no plans we can make to deal with the unexpected, but we can prepare ourselves. We can develop greater stability within, so that the unexpected does not arouse our fears and throw us so easily; and we can foster a greater inner flexibility, so that we can respond to changes with presence of mind rather than through the patterns of the past.

Then, as we begin to gain a greater inner stability and equanimity in this changeful world, we may find the courage to express our deeper values and use our technology to create the world we really want. Perhaps then the global brain can develop a global heart.

Peter Russell
London, 1994

INVITATION

I would like you to come with me on a great adventure, an exploration of humanity's potential as seen through the eyes of the planet, and to share with me a vision of our evolutionary future. The journey will take us beyond this place and time, allowing us to stand back and behold humanity afresh, to consider new ways of seeing ourselves in relation to the whole evolutionary process.

We shall see that something miraculous may be taking place on this planet, on this blue pearl of ours. Humanity could be on the threshold of an evolutionary leap, a leap that could occur in a flash of evolutionary time, a leap such as occurs only once in a billion years. The changes leading to this leap are taking place right before our eyes—or rather right behind them, within our minds.

Put as bluntly as this, the hypothesis might seem to be an unbelievable fantasy. Yet I hope to show that it could be a very real possibility, a possibility that an increasing number of people are beginning to take seriously.

The seeds of my own explorations in this area were sown some thirty years ago while I was a student in high school.

I can recall lying in bed one night, looking out at a starlit sky, and considering the rapidly increasing human population and the many ways in which we were consuming scarce resources and polluting the planet. It was no great effort to extrapolate these trends into the future and see that sooner or later impossible situations would occur. (To take an obvious example, there would eventually come a time when there would be more people alive than it was physically possible to feed.) But impossible situations do not occur, I reasoned. Therefore, before such points in time were reached, humanity would experience some very dramatic changes. Whatever happened, we would not continue on this path of continual growth much longer.

In retrospect, the conclusion was hardly profound, but for me it was an important turning point. It became very clear that during my lifetime I would probably witness the end of a set of trends that had been going on for thousands of years.

How would the changes come? At the time my attention was occupied with various negative scenarios such as nuclear holocaust, ecological collapse, or worldwide famine. These all seemed quite possible ways in which humanity's growing size and consumption could be curtailed, halted, or even reversed.

But gradually over the years another, more optimistic scenario began to dawn within my mind. Rather than humanity suffering major setbacks, the dramatic change could be a growing up and maturing of our species.

By this time I was at Cambridge University studying theoretical physics. Fascinated as I was by science, however, I was even more fascinated by the workings of the mind. Western philosophy and psychology seemed to offer a few insights, but I had felt for a long time that there was a vast amount of wisdom locked up in the East, in particular in various teachings on meditation. I ended up spending a winter in the Himalayan foothills, studying with Maharishi Mahesh Yogi and experiencing dimensions to consciousness of which I had never dreamed. As a result, I knew beyond any doubt that if everyone could contact such states of consciousness, the world would be transformed. Humanity could change its direction constructively, rather than be changed destructively. I returned to England and spent much of the next few years teaching meditation, encouraging others to discover for themselves a different way of being.

My vision of a transformed world continued to evolve, though for a while I felt very much on my own. Then one day a friend introduced me to the world of Teilhard de Chardin. Here was a philosopher who had considered similar ideas about humanity's future, considered them far more deeply, and had not been universally dismissed. I felt both inspired and strengthened.

From then on support started coming from many different directions: from developments in a number of sciences, from the writings of philosophers and visionaries both Eastern and Western, from conversations with others, and from my own experiences and insights. Piece by piece the jigsaw was coming together, and an overall picture began to emerge. More and more it appeared that we alive today might be standing on the threshold of an evolutionary development as significant as the emergence of life on Earth some 3,500 million years ago.

The nature of this possible transformation and the ways in which it could come about are what I want to explore with you in this book.

Our inquiry will draw upon the insights and experiences of many individuals, from mystics and religious teachers to scientists and astronauts, as well as on recent developments in many different disciplines. Biology, chemistry, physics, astronomy, psychology, physiology, medicine, sociology, technology, cybernetics, and systems theory will all shed their appropriate lights.

At times we will be looking at the similarities between aspects of society today and various phenomena in these sciences. In most cases these are not just analogies introduced to make a point clearer: they illustrate a deeper, underlying pattern, what is technically called a homology. (The layout of bones in the forearm of a dog, elephant, seal, and bat, for example, is in each case similar to the layout in the human forearm. This is a homology revealing a more fundamental common pattern.) When we start finding consistent, underlying patterns running through the whole of evolution, they can give us a very strong reason for believing that society today may follow homologous developments.

No extrapolation into the future can ever be watertight, and the material that follows is not meant to constitute a prediction or scientific proof. Rather, it is supporting evidence, providing a context within which an evolutionary leap would appear to be a possibility and worth exploring further.

My goal is to convey a vision as a whole. It is the overall picture that is important, not specific details. You may not like or agree with every point; indeed I would not expect you to accept everything. Nor need the picture that emerges for you be the same as mine. You will probably start making connections with your own knowledge and experience. My purpose is to set you thinking about positive alternative futures.

The vision I shall be sharing may seem a very optimistic one—some might even say Utopian—and I make no apologies for this. As will become clear later, the image a society has of itself can play a crucial role in the shaping of its future. If we fill our minds with images of gloom and destruction, then that is likely to be the way we are headed. Conversely, more optimistic attitudes can actually help promote a better world. A positive vision is like the light at the end of a tunnel, which, even though dimly glimpsed, encourages us to step on in that direction.

ACKNOWLEDGMENTS

When I began this book, I thought I had the ideas and structure all sewn up and that in six months, or a year at the most, I would see it finished. Three-and-a-half years later hardly a day had passed when the book had not occupied me in one way or another. My reading continually brought to light more information, conversations with friends sparked new ideas and insights, and in my quieter periods new syntheses suddenly appeared. Rather than being written, the book evolved, which is perhaps appropriate for a book whose main theme is evolution.

The new data, the new inspirations, and the new syntheses could go on forever. But then, six revisions after the first, the time came to put down my pen and let you, the reader, have a turn at playing with some of the ideas and sharing in some of my excitement.

With such a book as this it is impossible to give credit to everyone who has helped in one way or another over the course of its development, not to mention the many who influenced my thinking long before the book was ever conceived. In particular, I am indebted to Maharishi Mahesh Yogi and the knowledge he has shared over the years. He was a crucial catalyst to my own thinking, and, without his wisdom and my experiences with meditation, I probably never would have started this venture.

A number of other writers, both past and present, have greatly influenced my work. Those to whom I probably owe the most are Teilhard de Chardin, Sri Aurobindo, Walter Stace, Lancelot Law Whyte, Alan Watts, and Olaf Stapledon. Since I have not set out to write a scientific thesis, I have not punctuated every fact or example with its academic heritage; instead I have included a "Further Reading" section at the end in which all the relevant books are listed, together with a short description of each one. I hope these books will be as great a source of inspiration to the reader as they have been to me.

I must also credit that ordering principle within the universe that manifests itself to us as synchronicity. Many times in my conversations and readings I find the same ideas and insights cropping up in different minds around the planet. It seems that when the time is ripe an idea will sweep through the collective unconscious appearing simultaneously in many guises. In these situations it is impossible to credit any one person as the "originator"; it is the cosmic creative intelligence, the pulse of evolution, that should be credited.

Special thanks must go to Jeremy Tarcher, the publisher of the first American edition, both for his enthusiasm and for far exceeding any writer's expectations of a publisher in constantly making sure everything was as clear as it could be. He remains one of the most considerate and caring publishers I have ever met. Then I must also thank the late Stephanie E. Bernstein, who flew from Los Angeles to England on behalf of Jeremy to spend two weeks helping me put the finishing touches to the final version (braving an English summer and my own style of "simple" living). She ended up staying seven weeks, and as a result another final version emerged. Painful though the process was at times, we saw it through, and it was worth it. Meanwhile my British publisher waited patiently.

Many others helped at various times. Mary Douglas, who one day got me to stop talking about the book and actually start writing, encouraged me throughout. Guy Dauncey, Michael Carey, Ned and Tinker Beatty, Ruth Bender, Mark Brown, Karen Brown, John St. John, Trevor Williams, Jane Henry, and Norrie Huddle each gave me valuable criticism and feedback on the manuscript in various stages of its evolution. Marion Russell, in addition to giving constant feedback, was a continual source of support, helping me through the writer's blues with kindness, understanding, and patience. Thanks also to the numerous other friends who encouraged me to keep going—usually with cries of "I want a copy, now!" And last, but not least, I am especially grateful to Pat Masters, who was prepared to work till all hours when I suddenly unloaded a pile of work upon her, and who, having typed and retyped the book many times, now knows parts of it by heart.

The second edition of the book has been published by Global Brain, Inc. You may wonder how that came to be. A few years back Orion Kopelman picked up a tattered copy of the first edition in a used book store and was so inspired by what he read that he decided to establish a company dedicated to synergizing technology and consciousness and so make the global brain a reality. The updated edition of *The Global Brain Awakens* seemed a most appropriate publication for the company to produce, and offered me the opportunity to be more involved in the process than with a regular publisher. Over the last year Orion's enthusiasm and commitment have been invaluable in bringing this updated edition into being. His assistant, Danielle LaPorte, became my new editor, providing greatly appreciated support through the various stages of the book's production.

Finally, a comment regarding the *he* dilemma: current alternatives such as *e, s/he, hesh, co, tey, de, he'er, thon, jhe, per* or *wen*, and even the continual use of "he or she", tend to break the reader's flow. So, in order to keep the reading as smooth as possible, I have in places used *he* in its androgynous sense of "he or she".

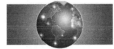 PART ONE

THE BIGGER PICTURE

CHAPTER 1

NEW VIEWS OF EARTH

> Once a photograph of the Earth, taken from the
> outside, is available . . . a new idea as powerful
> as any in history will let loose.
> *Sir Fred Hoyle, 1948*

What is home? To a man visiting a neighbor across the road, home is his house, his rose bushes, his backyard. To the peasant bringing goods to the city, it is his village. To the traveler abroad, it is his country. These are common human experiences. At one time or another, we each have called our town, state, or nation "home". Yet there is a greater home that has only recently come into our awareness, even though it has been ours all along: planet Earth.

As the first astronauts traveled out into space and the

Earth receded into the distance, national boundaries began to lose their significance. These space pioneers no longer found themselves identifying with a particular country, class, or race, but with humanity and the planet as a whole. Standing on the lunar surface, the astronauts saw what no human being has ever seen before: the great sphere that is Earth, four times as big and five times as bright as the moon itself.

To Edgar Mitchell, the sixth man to stand on the moon, this was a deeply moving experience, and he felt a strong connection to the planet. "It was a beautiful, harmonious, peaceful-looking planet, blue with white clouds, and one that gave you a deep sense... of home, of being, of identity. It is what I prefer to call instant global consciousness."

Mitchell observed that everyone who has been to the moon has had similar experiences. "Each man comes back with a feeling that he is no longer an American citizen—he is a planetary citizen."

Russell Schweickart, another astronaut, similarly felt a profound change in his relationship to the planet.

> You realize that on that small spot, that little blue and white thing, is everything that means anything to you — all of history and music and poetry and art and death and birth and love, tears, joy, games — all of it on that little spot out there. . . . You recognize that you are a piece of this total life. . . . And when you come back there is a difference in that world now. There is a difference in that relationship between you and that planet and you and all those other forms of life on that planet, because you've had that kind of experience.

But the astronauts were not the only ones to have experienced this profound change of perspective. The photographs of our planet brought back from space triggered similar deep reactions in many Earthbound men and women, feelings of awe and connectedness.

The profound impact of this earth view has resulted in this picture being used in almost every sphere of human activity. It adorns the walls of offices and living rooms; it is on greeting cards, T-shirts, and bumper stickers. Ecological movements and planetary organizations incorporate it in their logos, as do educational institutions and business corporations. At one time or another it has been used to advertise just about everything from cars, washing machines, and shoes, to book clubs, banks, and insurance companies. Yet in spite of all this exposure, the picture still strikes a very deep chord, and none of its magnificence has been lost.

It is not entirely coincidental that this photograph achieved its widespread appeal at the same time that many people were becoming increasingly concerned about the relationship between humanity and the planet and our need to live in harmony with each other and with our environment. The picture has become a spiritual symbol for our times. It stands for the growing awareness that we and the planet are all part of a single system, that we can no longer divorce ourselves from the whole.

So the most valuable spin-off from the moon expeditions may have been, not in the field of science, economics, politics, or the military, but in the field of consciousness. Getting to the moon allowed humanity for the first time to look upon this blue pearl that has been our home for millions of years and to see it as a whole. As Edgar Mitchell pointed out, "The payoff from Apollo may be inestimably richer than anyone anticipated."

A Living Earth?

Another thought that struck some of the early astronauts was the possibility that the planet as a whole might be a living being. We Earthlings could be likened to fleas who spend their whole lives on an elephant. They chart its terrain—skin, hairs, and bumps—study its chemistry, plot its temperature changes, and classify the other animals that share their world, arriving at a reasonable perception of where they live. Then one day a few of the fleas take a huge leap and look at the elephant from a distance of a hundred feet. Suddenly it dawns: "The whole thing is alive!" This is the truly awesome realization brought about by the trip to the moon. The whole planet appears to be alive— not just teeming with life but an organism in its own right.

If the idea of the Earth as a *living being* is initially difficult to accept, it may be due partly to our assumptions about what sorts of things can and cannot be organisms. We accept a vast range of systems as living organisms, from bacteria to blue whales, but when it comes to the whole planet we might find this concept a bit hard to grasp. But we should remember that before the development of the microscope (less than four hundred years ago), few people realized that there were living organisms within us and around us, so small that they cannot be seen with the na-

ked eye. Today we are viewing life from the other direction, through the "macroscope" of the Earth view, and we
are beginning to surmise that something as vast as our planet
could also be a living organism.

To better understand the planet as a living system, we
need to go beyond the time scales of human life to the
planet's own time scale, vastly greater than our own. Looked
at in this way, the rhythm of day and night might be the
pulse of the planet, one full cycle for every hundred thousand human heartbeats. Speeding up time appropriately,
we would see the atmosphere and ocean currents swirling
round the planet, circulating nutrients and carrying away
waste products, much as the blood circulates nutrients and
carries away waste in our own bodies.

Speeding it up a hundred million more times, we would
see the vast continents sliding around, bumping into each
other, pushing up great mountain chains where they col-
lide. Fine, threadlike rivers would swing first one way then
another, developing huge, meandering loops as they accommodate themselves to the changes in the land. Giant forests
and grasslands would move across the continents, sometimes thrusting limbs into new fertile lands and at other
times withdrawing as climate and soil change.

If we could look inside, we would see an enormous
churning current of liquid rock flowing back and forth between the center of the planet and the thin crust, sometimes
oozing through volcanic pores to supply the minerals essential for life.

Had we senses able to detect charged particles, we would
see the planet bathing not only in the light and heat of the
sun but also in a solar wind of ions streaming from the sun.

This wind, flowing round the Earth, would be shaped by her magnetic field into a huge, pulsating aura streaming off into space behind her for millions of miles. Changes in the Earth's fluctuating magnetic state would be visible as ripples and colors in this vast comet-like aura, and the Earth herself would be but a small blue-green sphere at the head of this vast energy field.

Such similarities show a level of complex activity similar to that found in a living organism. They do not, however, constitute any form of scientific proof. The question we have to ask is whether science could accept the planet as a single living system in the same way it accepts bacteria and whales?

Today this no longer seems so farfetched. On the contrary, an increasingly popular scientific hypothesis suggests that the most satisfactory way of understanding the planet's chemistry, ecology, and biology is to view the planet as a single living system.

CHAPTER 2

THE GAIA HYPOTHESIS

> We are natural creatures which have evolved
> inside a great life system. Whatever we do that
> is not good for life, the rest of the system will try
> to undo or balance in any way it can.
>
> *Elisabet Sahtouris*

O ne of the major proponents of the theory that the planet behaves like a living system is British chemist and inventor Dr. James Lovelock. His ideas, which have fundamentally altered many people's perception of the planet, were another fortuitous spin-off from the space race.

In the early 1960s Lovelock served as a consultant to a team at the California Institute of Technology working on plans for the investigation of life on Mars. One problem they faced in looking for Martian life-forms was not knowing exactly what they were looking for. Other life-forms might be based on completely different chemistries—on silicon rather than carbon, for instance—and might not reveal themselves to tests based on Earthly life.

Lovelock theorized that however strange the chemistry and life-form might be, there would be one very general characteristic: any life-form would take in, process, and cast out matter and energy, and this would have detectable effects upon its physical surroundings. On a planet devoid of life, the chemical constituents of its atmosphere, oceans, and soil, through their interactions over millions of years, would settle into equilibrium; the proportions of the various constituents could be predicted roughly by the laws of physical chemistry. If, however, life were present, then whatever chemical processes it was based on almost certainly would leave the environment in a state recognizably different from that predicted by physical chemistry alone.

As a very simple example of this principle, consider a jar containing a mixture of sugar and water. Physical chemistry predicts that the sugar will dissolve until a given concentration is reached. If life in the form of yeast cells were added and left to grow, however, the resulting mix would be very different: there would be a lower concentration of sugar than predicted and much higher levels of alcohol and other organic products. We would determine, then, whether there was (or had been) life in the jar by measuring the sugar and alcohol concentrations.

The beauty of Lovelock's approach to life detection is that one need not visit another planet to know whether or not life is there. The basic chemistry of the atmosphere can be deduced from Earthbound examination of the infrared, light, and radio waves coming from the planet. In the 1960s enough was known about the Martian atmosphere to suggest that it was very close to the state of chemical equilibrium; it showed no signs of the exotic chemistry characteristic of the presence of life. So, Lovelock concluded, it was extremely unlikely that there was life on Mars.

Applying a similar approach to the atmosphere, oceans, and soil of our own planet, Lovelock found that the chemical constituents were far removed from equilibrium. To the casual observer it might seem that he had merely shown that there was, after all, life on Earth. But Lovelock began to see far greater significance in these disequilibria.

First, the concentration of gases in the Earth's atmosphere differs by factors of millions from the levels predicted by physical chemistry. The predicted level of oxygen in the air, for example, would be virtually zero, yet the actual concentration is about 21 percent. This is puzzling because oxygen is a highly reactive gas, combining readily with many other chemical elements; it should therefore be rapidly absorbed. Second, and even more puzzling, the actual composition of the atmosphere has for eons remained at a level that is optimal for the continuance of life.

After pondering many such unlikely characteristics, Lovelock came to "the only feasible explanation": the atmosphere is being manipulated on a day-to-day basis by the many living processes on Earth. The entire range of living matter on Earth, from viruses to whales, from algae to oaks, plus the air, the oceans, and the land surface, all appear to be a part of a giant system able to regulate the temperature and composition of the air, sea, and soil so as to ensure the survival of life. This concept Lovelock termed the "Gaia Hypothesis" in honor of the ancient Greek "Earth Mother", *Gaia* (or *Ge*). In this context Gaia signifies the entire biosphere—everything living on the planet—plus the atmosphere, the oceans, and the soil.

In maintaining the optimal conditions for life, Gaia manifests a characteristic that all living systems have in common: homeostasis. Derived from the Greek for "to keep the same", the term was coined by Claude Bernard, a nineteenth-century French physiologist, who stated that "all the vital mechanisms, varied as they are, have only one object: that of preserving constant the conditions of life."

An example of homeostasis is the human body's maintenance of a temperature of about 98.6 degrees Fahrenheit, the ideal temperature for the majority of the body's processes. Although the external temperature may vary by scores of degrees, our internal temperature seldom varies by more than a degree or two, the body cooling itself through sweating and warming itself through physical activity and shivering. The regulation of the number of white blood cells, the control of acidity, salt content, and the delicate chemical balance of the blood are homeostatic processes as well. These and many others maintain the best internal environment for the continuance of your body's life processes. Such processes are found not only in the human body and in all living systems but also within Gaia herself.

Gaia appears to maintain planetary homeostasis in a variety of ways, monitoring and modifying many key components in the atmosphere, oceans, and soil. The data that Lovelock amassed in support of this contention is fascinating, and the interested reader should take a look at Lovelock's book, *Gaia: A New Look at Life on Earth*, and his sequel, *The Ages of Gaia*.   In summary, some of the indications of Gaia's homeostatic mechanisms are:

The steadiness of the Earth's surface temperature: Although life is found to exist between the extremes of 20 and 220 degrees Fahrenheit, the optimal range is between 60 and 100 degrees Fahrenheit. The average temperature of most of the Earth's surface appears to have stayed within this range for hundreds of millions of years despite major changes in atmospheric composition and an increase in the heat received from the sun. If at any time in the Earth's history the overall temperature had gone beyond these limits, life, as we know it, would have been extinguished.

The regulation of the amount of salt in the oceans: At present the oceans contain about 3.4 percent salt, and geological evidence shows that this figure has remained relatively constant, despite the fact that salt is being washed in continually by the rivers. If the salt concentration had ever risen as high as 4 percent, life in the sea would have evolved very differently. If it had exceeded 6 percent, even for a few minutes, life in the oceans immediately would have come to an end, for at this level of salinity cell walls disintegrate. The oceans would have become like the Dead Sea.

The stabilization of the oxygen concentration of the atmosphere at 21 percent: This is the optimal balance for the maintenance of life. With a few percent less oxygen, the larger animals and flying insects could not have found enough energy to survive; with a few percent more, even damp vegetation would burn. (A forest fire started by lightning would burn fiercely and indefinitely, eventually burning all vegetation on the Earth's land surface.)

The presence of a small quantity of ammonia in the atmosphere: This is the amount needed to neutralize the strong sulfuric and nitric acids produced by the natural combination of sulfur and nitrogen compounds with oxygen. (Thunderstorms, for instance, produce tons of nitric acid.) The result is that rain and soil remain at the optimal levels of acidity for the preservation of life.

The existence of the ozone layer in the upper atmosphere: This shields life on the surface from ultraviolet radiation, which damages the molecules essential for life, particularly the DNA molecules found in every living cell. Without it life on land is impossible.

On the basis of these and other "homeostatic" behaviors, Lovelock concludes that the climate and chemical properties of the Earth seem always to have been optimal for life as we know it.

Critics of the Gaia Hypothesis might argue that the origin and maintenance of life on this planet have resulted from a series of very lucky coincidences, rather than planetary homeostatic behavior. If, for example, the proportion of ammonia in the early atmosphere had been a little higher or lower, the Earth would have ended up too hot or too cold for life. They might argue that it has been a series of flukes that kept the planet's surface temperature roughly constant while the sun's output changed; a series of flukes that kept the levels of carbon dioxide, oxygen, salt and many other chemicals at optimal levels for the maintenance of life; and a fluke that there is an ozone layer to protect us from lethal quantities of ultraviolet light.

In the same way, a cell in the human body, observing the body's continued survival through heat, cold, and many other changes, might, if it were so inclined, put it all down to a series of lucky coincidences; the body just happens to sweat when it is hot, just happens to shiver when it is cold, just happens to take in the right amount of nutrients when they are needed. Perhaps by a fluke, blood sugar, acidity, and salinity stay at the optimal levels and red blood cells happen to bring along oxygen and take away wastes. From such a point of view, the body survives from one moment to the next as a result of an extremely fortunate series of coincidences.

This quite definitely is not the case. The body behaves in a well-ordered manner with a definite sense of purpose. It sweats, shivers, eats, breathes, and regulates its internal functions and chemical constituents in order to preserve homeostasis, and so survive.

Just as this self-regulating principle makes more sense of the body's activities, so it makes more sense of the planet's. Gaia appears to be a self-regulating system, continually adjusting its chemical, physical, and biological processes in order to support life in its continuing evolution.

Does the Gaia Hypothesis imply that the biosphere is a single living organism? Lovelock is cautious on this point. He sees the atmosphere to be similar to a beehive, a biological construction designed to maintain a chosen environment, though not actually living in itself. But if we take the atmosphere, oceans, and soil to be intrinsic parts of a complete biosystem, couldn't we then speculate that the system as a whole is alive? And if so, is humanity an intricate, inseparable part of a larger living system? Before we can answer these questions, we need to look more closely at the general characteristics common to all living systems and see to what extent Gaia satisfies them.

CHAPTER 3

LIVING SYSTEMS THEORY

> The major problems of our time are systemic;
> They cannot be understood in isolation. They
> need a systemic, or holistic, approach to be solved.
> *Fritjof Capra*

Until the middle of this century, each scientific subject was treated as a more or less isolated field: physiologists studied the body, sociologists studied social groups, and engineers studied mechanical systems. Each discipline had its own theories, and these generally had very little connection with the findings of other sciences. In the late 1940s, however, biologists, such as Ludwig von Bertalanffy and Paul Weiss, began to change this by focusing on the common principles and properties underlying widely varied phenomena.

The concept of homeostasis, for example, originally applied to physiological processes, was extended by von Bertalanffy to encompass a much wider range of phenomena—from single cells to whole populations. Similarly, the concept of feedback, which originally came from engineering, was seen to be applicable to physiological, psychological, and social phenomena. The insights gained from developing general models provided the impetus for an interdisciplinary field now known as General Systems Theory.

The term *theory* is somewhat misleading. General Systems Theory is not so much a specific theory as a way of looking at the world. It suggests that the world is an interconnected hierarchy of matter and energy. According to this view, nothing can really be understood on its own; everything is part of a system (a set of interrelating, interacting units). Systems may be abstract, as in mathematical and metaphysical systems, or concrete, as in telephone or transport systems.

One branch of General Systems Theory deals in particular with living systems. In his magnum opus, *Living Systems*, James Miller, one of the pioneers of this approach, proposed that all living systems are composed of subsystems that take in, process, and put out matter, energy, or information, or combinations of these. He identified nineteen critical subsystems that seem to characterize living systems, and found that they applied to both biological systems and social systems.

The first eight subsystems are concerned with matter-energy processes and portray the way any living system ingests, digests, uses, and excretes physical matter and energy. All living systems, for example, have an "ingestor", some means of taking in matter and energy, whether it be a gap in a cell wall, an artery leading into an organ, the mouth of an organism, or a major seaport.

The next nine subsystems are concerned with information processes, the ways in which living systems sense the environment, abstract information, integrate, store, and retrieve it. An example of such a subsystem is the "input transducer", which brings information into the system. This may be the receptor site in the membrane of a nerve cell, the eye of an organism, or the foreign news service of a nation.

The last two subsystems involve both matter-energy and information processes. The "reproducer" leads to the creation of new systems similar to its own, through the transmission of both physical matter and information about the original system. The "boundary" holds the whole system together, excluding or permitting the entry or exit of various types of matter, energy, and information.

Looking at the entire biosystem from the perspective of General Living Systems Theory, we can find each of the nineteen critical subsystems at work. For example, the planetary ingestors are both the upper atmosphere, through which the sun's energy and cosmic dust are taken in, and the Earth's crust, through which minerals well up. The input transducers are the many plants and animals as they react to daily and seasonal changes or to earthquakes and sunspot activity. Table 1 outlines the nineteen subsystems in relation to both the human body and the biosphere. It also shows how they apply to a human society, a point we shall be returning to later.

Table 1. The nineteen subsystems of a general living system, with examples at the level of the human body, human society, and the biosphere. (These examples are by no means exhaustive; many others can be found.)

SUBSYSTEM	LEVEL *Human Body*	*Human Society* *(a nation)*	*Biosphere (Gaia)*
Ingestor: Brings matter-energy across boundary from outside	Mouth, nose and lungs	Import company, Airlines	Atmosphere (transparent to visible light and infrared, and permitting cosmic dust to fall through) Volcanoes (permitting flow of minerals through Earth's crust)
Distributor: Carries matter-energy around the system	Blood	Transport company, Oil pipeline	Temperature and pressure gradients in atmosphere and oceans Animal migrations and wandering
Converter: Changes certain inputs into more useful forms	Teeth, stomach, small intestine, liver, pancreas	Oil refinery, Farm	Mosses and lichens converting minerals to humus Plants photosynthesizing light into chemical bonds
Producer: Forms stable associations among inputs, or outputs, of converter, for growth, repair, movement	Protein synthesis by RNA., Production of new skin by epidermis	Factory, Construction company	Producers occur at cellular level, e.g., chloroplasts, mitochondria, RNA, and in reproduction of each species
Matter-Energy: Storage	Fatty tissues, calcium in bones	Warehouses, Dammed rivers	Dead plant and animal matter in soil Water in oceans and atmosphere
Extruder: Transmits waste matter-energy out of system	Urethra, anus, lungs	Export company, Smokestacks, Refuse collectors	Sedimentation in oceans Gaseous escape through upper atmosphere
Motor: Moves system, or parts of it, or moves environments	Muscles	Cars, trains, boats, planes	Tides Climate changes Continental drift
Supporter: Maintains proper spatial structure	Skeleton	Housing, Public buildings	Earth's crust, Buoyancy of air and sea
Input Transducer: Sensory receptors for information coming from outside	Eyes, ears, heat sensors	Foreign news service, Scientific research	Animals and plants reacting to day and night, to seasons and earthquakes
Internal Transducer: Receives information about changes going on within system	Hypothalamus in brain monitoring temperature, salt content of blood	Public opinion polls, Political parties	Animal and plant reactions to changing climate, floods, aridity, pollution

Table 1. (*continued*)

Channel and Net: Routes by which information transmitted to all parts of system	Central and peripheral nervous system, Hormonal system	Books, magazines, telephones, TV, Postal services, conferences	Animal migration and wandering, Seed dispersal in plants, Availability of food
Decoder: Translation of input information into internal meaningful code	Retina of eye, Visual cortex of brain	Translators, Commentators, Foreign Office	Interspecies communication - to response to reactions of other living beings
Associator: Associates items of information, the first stage of the learning process	Temporal and frontal lobes of the brain	Scholars	Changed habitats and behaviors
Memory: Stores various types of information over different periods of time	Entire brain	Libraries, Data banks	Evolutionary adaptations recorded in changed genes
Decider: Receives information from other subsystems and transmits to them information controlling entire system	Various brain centers, Spinal chord, Pituitary gland	Governments, Law courts, Voting public	Soil, Interspecies communication
Encoder: Translates internal information to external messages	Speech area of brain	Newspapers	Changes in constituents of atmosphere
Output Transducer: Changes information into other matter-energy forms and transmits them into environment	Voice box, facial expressions	TV station, Official spokesman	Upper atmosphere, gaseous loss and radiation, changed albedo (reflectivity) of planet
Reproducer: Gives rise to similar systems	Sexual organs	Settlers abroad, Social reformers	Viruses lost to space, Interplanetary travel
Boundary: Holds system together, protects from external stresses, excludes or permits various inputs and outputs	Skin	Customs officials, National border	Earth's crust below, Upper atmosphere above

But does the fact that the biosphere appears to possess each of the nineteen subsystems characteristic of life prove that it is indeed a living system? These subsystems may all be necessary characteristics, but are they *sufficient*? The answer is almost certainly no. An automobile displays many of these characteristics and, with various modifications and additions, could be made to satisfy them all, but even then it would not be a living system.

There is one more characteristic common to all living systems that clearly distinguishes them from non-living systems. This is a living system's ability to maintain a high degree of internal order despite a continually changing environment (something we shall be looking at in depth in Chapter 5). Machines generally do not show this characteristic. They wear out and run down; they are not self-organizing. Since few (if any) non-living systems possess the nineteen critical subsystems and are self-organizing as well, satisfaction of both these criteria seems to be sufficient to define a living system.

Gaia appears to satisfy both criteria. Her self-organizing nature has been well explored in Lovelock's work on planetary homeostasis. Gaia also satisfies Miller's criteria. Taken together, these two findings suggest that Gaia could be considered to be a living system in her own right.

HUMANITY IN GAIA

If we postulate that the entire biosphere has evolved as a single living system, in which all the numerous subsystems play diverse and mutually dependent roles, then humanity, a subsystem of this larger planetary system, cannot be separated from it or treated in isolation. What then might be our function in relationship to Gaia?

One possible response to this question suggests that humanity is like some vast nervous system, a global brain in which each of us is an individual nerve cell. Human society can be seen as one enormous data-collection, data-communication, and data-memory system. We have grouped ourselves into clusters of cities and towns rather like nerve cells clustered into ganglia on a vast nervous system. Linking the "ganglia" and the individual "nerve cells" are vast information networks.

Society's slower systems of communication, such as the postal service, are like the relatively slow chemical communication networks of the body, such as the hormonal system. Our faster, electronically based telecommunications networks (telephones, radio, computer networks) are like the billions of tiny fibers linking the nerve cells in the brain.

At any instant there are millions of messages flashing through the global network, just as in the human brain countless messages are continually flashing back and forth. Our various libraries of books, tapes, and other records can be seen as part of the collective memory of Gaia. Through language and science we have been able to understand much of what happens around us, monitoring the planet's behavior much as the brain monitors the body's. And humanity's search for knowledge could be Gaia's way of knowing more about herself and the universe in which she lives.

Many of the above parallels relate to the higher mental functions, to thinking, knowing, perceiving, and understanding. These are functions associated with the cortex of the human brain, the thin layer of nerve cells wrapped around the outside of the brain; so it might be more accurate to liken humanity to the cortex of the planet. In evolutionary terms, the cortex is a relatively late addition, most of its development occurring with the mammals. It is not necessary for the maintenance of life. The cortex of an animal can be removed, yet the circulation, breathing, digestion, and metabolism continue. In a similar way, the planet Earth survived perfectly well without humanity for over 4,000 million years and possibly could continue very well without it.

There is, however, a second, very different response to the question of humanity's role in Gaia. We might be some form of recently erupted, malignant growth, which the planet would be better off without. This possibility occurred to Edgar Mitchell while standing on the moon. Immediately after feeling a sense of identity with the planet as a whole, came the opposite feeling, "that beneath that blue and white atmosphere was a growing chaos that the inhabitants of planet Earth were breeding among themselves—the population and technology were growing rapidly out of control. The crew of 'spacecraft Earth' was in virtual mutiny to the order of the Universe."

Modern civilization does indeed seem to be eating its way across the surface of the planet, consuming in decades resources that Gaia herself inherited billions of years ago, and threatening the biological fabric that took millennia to create. Large forests essential to the ecosystem are looking moth-eaten, animal species are being hunted out of existence, lakes and rivers are turning sour, and enormous areas of the planet are being made barren by mining and the spread of concrete. Indeed, an aerial photograph of almost any large metropolis with its sprawling suburbs is very reminiscent of the way some cancers grow in the human body. Technological civilization looks like a rampant malignant growth blindly devouring its own ancestral host in a selfish act of consumption.

But perhaps these two views of humanity's role in Gaia are not opposing. Perhaps we *are* some kind of embryonic global brain, *and,* at a very critical stage in its development, this planetary nervous system is getting out of control, threatening to destroy the very body that supports its existence.

If we are to fulfill our role as a part of a planetary brain, our malignant behavior must be stopped. To bring this about, we will need to change, in the most radical way, our attitudes toward ourselves, others, and the planet as a whole. To appreciate what such a transformation could mean, both for humanity and for Gaia, and how it could come about, it will be valuable to look first to our past, at the whole evolutionary process. As we look at its underlying principles and significant developments, we may gain a clearer idea of where we are headed.

PART TWO

EVOLUTION PAST, PRESENT, AND FUTURE

CHAPTER 4

EVOLUTION SO FAR

Matter has reached the point of beginning to
know itself. . . . [Man is] a star's way of knowing
about stars.

George Wald

What do we mean by evolution? To most people the
word probably signifies the gradual development
of the many living species, probably along the lines that
Charles Darwin proposed in his treatise *On the Origin of
Species*. Here, however, we shall be considering evolution
in a broader context. We shall be going back in time to
consider the unfolding of the universe long before life appeared and to look at the origin and development of matter
itself, for without this earlier evolution, life could never
have started. Later we shall be stepping into the future to

explore what developments might lie beyond the evolution of human beings. From this perspective, the evolution of life may be but an act in a far grander cosmic play. But let us start at the beginning, with the origins of the universe itself.

How did the universe begin? Did it even have a beginning? Many theories have been advanced, some based on physical science, others based on spiritual, metaphysical, or philosophical frameworks. At present the most widely accepted theory in the West is the scientific model that suggests that the universe started from some huge cosmic explosion.

In 1922 the Russian mathematician Alexandre Friedmann showed that Einstein's Theory of Relativity predicted an expanding universe rather than a static one. Seven years later the American astronomer Edwin Hubble discovered that this was indeed the case. All the galaxies appeared to be rushing away from each other, as if thrown apart by some great explosion in the past. In the 1950s three British astronomers, Fred Hoyle, Hermann Bondi, and Thomas Gould, proposed that this continued expansion might be explained by the continuous creation of matter throughout space, in which case the universe could have been going on forever. Although many found this "steady state" theory to be intellectually more satisfying, it has not been supported by further research. Rather, the weight of the evidence gathered over the last three decades has strongly favored the idea of the universe having begun with a "Big Bang" some ten to fifteen billion years ago. According to this view, the whole universe as we know it was born from a gigantic superhot fireball, which rapidly expanded and cooled, condensing over billions of years into countless galaxies and a myriad of stars.

Drawing on developments and discoveries in mathematics, physics, and astronomy, scientists today are beginning to paint a fairly detailed picture of what probably happened during this cosmic explosion. Of what happened before the Big Bang, physics has little to put forth. (Time and space only came into being once the process began—hard as that may be for us to grasp.) Nor is there any known physics to describe what happened in the first one-hundredth of a second of the Big Bang, when the temperature of the universe was well over a trillion degrees Fahrenheit, so hot that electrons, protons, and other elementary particles could not exist. The most science can say about the universe during this time is that it was a state of pure energy, dense with electromagnetic radiation. To borrow from another view of creation: In the beginning, there was Light.

These theories state that after the first one-hundredth of a second, the universe had cooled down sufficiently (to a hundred billion degrees Fahrenheit) for elementary particles—electrons, protons, and neutrons—to form. At this stage, the universe was expanding very fast, and cooling very rapidly. Yet it was still far too hot for any simple atomic nuclei to form, let alone make complete atoms. Any particles that did by chance come together to form nuclei would have been shaken apart instantly by the intense heat energy. Only after about three minutes had elapsed, when the universe had cooled down to about 1.6 billion degrees Fahrenheit, could neutrons and protons combine to form stable atomic nuclei—initially the nuclei of hydrogen and helium.

The universe continued to expand and cool until, after about 700,000 years, the temperature had decreased to around 7,000 degrees Fahrenheit, which is about the temperature of our sun. At this temperature, electrons and nuclei could stay together and so form complete simple atoms.

At the same time as the intense radiant heat energy was driving matter apart, the much weaker gravitational attraction of matter for matter was tending to pull it back together. Below 7,000 degrees Fahrenheit, the pressure of the radiant heat had decreased to the point where gravitational effects began to dominate and atoms began to clump together. Wherever atoms happened to be a little more densely clustered, they produced a slightly stronger gravitational field, attracting other atoms toward them. Slowly the irregularities were amplified and, over thousands of millions of years, these eddies became clusters of primordial galaxies. Within these giant clouds the hydrogen and helium gases continued to gather into more condensed masses, eventually giving birth to the first stars.

By this time the universe as a whole had become much colder—even by human standards—a few score degrees above absolute zero. As the cool gas was drawn into stars, however, it gained energy from the gravitational collapse. This, combined with the energy of the star's own radioactivity, heated the gas again to several million degrees.

Many of these early stars generated so much heat that they eventually flared up and exploded in brilliant supernovae, each as bright as an entire galaxy. The huge quantities of energy generated made it possible for nearly all the other chemical elements to form. Current theories of stellar evolution suggest that this process would have occurred as part of a thermonuclear chain reaction, and that within such supernovae 15 percent of the heavier elements would have been formed in ten seconds.

The force of the explosion sent these heavier elements spewing into space. Slowly, over millions of years, the debris condensed into new stars, forming yet more complex atoms. Later, these stars also exploded, spewing their material into space. This process has been repeated a number of times, and it is thought that our own sun is probably a fourth-generation star.

One consequence of this recycling and regeneration of matter is that every atom on this planet (with the possible exception of some hydrogen and helium left over from the Big Bang) has been processed in at least one star. Every atom in your body has passed through or been created in one of these giant stellar furnaces. And at some stage in its long history may have been in a volcano, in rocks, in the oceans, in the atmosphere, in an oak tree, in an eagle, and in other people past and present.

THE BUILDING BLOCKS OF LIFE

Before life could emerge, atoms had to combine to form molecules of increasing complexity. The stars themselves were far too hot for even the simplest molecules to form; the energy was such that any atoms that did come together were immediately flung apart again. The formation of a large variety of stable molecules needed the more moderate temperature ranges found in the regions around the stars.

Here, on the cooler planets, and perhaps in the surrounding space itself, atoms could begin to combine with each other to form simple molecules, substances such as water, carbon dioxide, and salts of various kinds. Our own solar system was probably formed about 4.6 billion years ago, from a huge cloud of interstellar dust. Most of the cloud was composed of frozen hydrogen, helium, and ice, but the planet Earth was fortunate to condense out of a part of the cloud rich in a diversity of elements, including all those necessary for the evolution of carbon-based life.

How life actually began is still a matter of considerable debate. The most popular model supposes that the early atmosphere consisted of a mixture of hydrogen, ammonia, methane, carbon dioxide, hydrogen sulfide, water vapor, and other simple gases formed from combinations of the lighter atoms. It is hypothesized that these gases could have combined to form life's essential chemical compounds. These combinations are stable at temperatures below the boiling point of water, and they could have formed as soon as the Earth's surface temperature fell below this level some 4 billion years ago—which, on the Earth's time scale, was not long after its birth.

Considerable support for this theory came from a now-classic experiment performed in 1953 by Stanley Miller, then a graduate student at the University of Chicago. In a flask in his laboratory he created a "primeval soup" of water, methane, nitrogen, ammonia, and traces of hydrogen which he subjected to electric sparks (simulating lightning). Within hours a large variety of organic substances such as sugars, aldehydes, carboxylic acids, and amino acids were formed—some of the basic components of life on this planet.

The experiment is so simple that it has since been repeated hundreds of times, even by high school students, with similar results. By varying the proportions of the different gases present, and by substituting ultraviolet light for electric discharges, subsequent researchers have found that all the basic building blocks of life can be created. Moreover, they can be created under a variety of different conditions. Further experiments have shown that it does not appear to be necessary to have a methane- and ammonia-rich atmosphere. The same molecules can also be built up in atmospheres rich in carbon dioxide and even in the icy cold of frozen oceans.

The fact that these chemicals are so easily created, and under so many different conditions, suggests that wherever these conditions are met—and probably billions of planets in the universe have passed through similar stages—the basic building blocks of life would almost certainly be created. And, their formation is not necessarily limited to planets. Experiments have shown that these basic molecules can form even in near-vacuums, at temperatures approaching absolute zero (the conditions found in interstellar space). Recently many of these compounds have indeed been detected way beyond our solar system.

That hydrogen and even helium occur throughout interstellar space has been known since the early days of radio astronomy, but until recently few people thought that more complex molecules existed out there. In 1965, however, cyanide (one atom of carbon connected to one of nitrogen) and the hydroxyl molecule (one atom of hydrogen plus one atom of oxygen) were detected in the gaseous clouds that lie in deep space. Spurred on by this result, a group of scientists led by Charles Townes at the University of California, Berkeley, began in 1968 to search for ammonia in space. They soon found it in the tenuous clouds of gas toward the center of our galaxy. As a bonus they also found water there. Shortly afterwards another team at the National Radio Astronomy Observatory in West Virginia detected formaldehyde throughout our galaxy, and later in many other galaxies. Since then, about one hundred organic molecules have been detected. More recently, in 1994, a team from the University of Illinois at Urbana-Champaign, discovered the amino acid glycine in a dense cloud of interstellar gas and dust near the center of our galaxy, and also found evidence of several other heavier molecules.

Two British astronomers, Fred Hoyle and Chandra Wickramsinghe, have argued in their book *Lifecloud* that on the tiny dust grains in the interstellar clouds, the conditions may well have been conducive to the formation of all the basic building blocks of life. If so, the seeds of life may have been universally available, cast upon the interstellar winds to fall on fertile planets as soon as they were formed.

Such hypotheses do not necessarily mean that life did not originate in the primeval soup; rather they suggest that these basic components of life could have come together in a variety of different ways—a kind of cosmic life ensurance policy. Furthermore it suggests that life is likely to be a widespread phenomenon throughout the universe, a natural consequence of chemical evolution.

THE EVOLUTION OF LIFE ON EARTH

The early oceans and rock pools of Earth were probably the setting for the next step in the evolutionary drama. Here the conditions were right for these chemicals—whether they originated on Earth or in interstellar space—to come together to form larger molecules such as amino acids, enzymes, and proteins. Over time these linked together into groups and chains of increasing complexity. Those that were more stable survived longer and combined with others to form yet larger units, macromolecules, some of them containing thousands of the basic building blocks and millions of atoms.

Some of these giant molecules developed the ability to "recognize" other smaller molecules. This was possible because each type of molecule had a specific three-dimensional shape; if a smaller molecule had a shape that fitted snugly into a nook in the more complex macromolecule, it could be "recognized" much as a key fits (or is recognized by) a lock. With this ability some macromolecules (in particular, deoxyribonucleic acid molecules—DNA) were able to arrange other smaller molecules into specific sequences. By building up sequences that were exact copies of themselves, they achieved the essence of reproduction.

Once complex, self-replicating organic molecules had established a stable hold, they began forming loose associations with other complex macromolecules. More and more molecules joined the groups, until eventually they reached a stage where the groups became integrated units. In this way the simplest cell was born 3.5 billion years ago.

These embryonic cells could not have survived for long

in the relatively chaotic environment in which they found themselves. Life probably emerged many times, only to be swallowed up again almost at once, much as any atomic nuclei formed in the primordial fireball would have been annihilated instantly by the superhot temperature. Biologists speculating on the origin of life generally believe that, over time, the process of repeated emergence and dissolution of life gradually built up a more hospitable environment, until a threshold was reached, beyond which the rate of creation exceeded the rate of loss. Life would then have established a stable foothold.

The first simple cells were algae and bacteria. They did not breathe oxygen; rather, they produced it through the process of photosynthesis and cast it away as a waste product. This oxygen became the first major pollutant on the planet. (To the organisms of the time, oxygen was as poisonous as chlorine is to us.) Initially, the free oxygen combined with minerals such as iron to produce various oxides, and as long as oxygen was absorbed in this way, life remained safe. After about a billion years, however, all the available iron had turned to rust, and oxygen began to accumulate in the atmosphere. At about the same time ultraviolet light—which earlier had been so valuable in the synthesis of amino acids, and thus necessary for the evolution of life—threatened to destroy the bacteria that had evolved.

Fortunately, this planetary crisis was averted. The extra oxygen combined to form a layer of ozone in the upper atmosphere, thereby preventing much of the ultraviolet light from reaching the planet's surface. Ingenuity triumphed, as James Lovelock points out, ". . .[not] in the human way by restoring the old order, but in the flexible Gaian way by adapting to change and converting a murderous intruder into a powerful friend."

As the oxygen continued to build up in the atmosphere, bacteria evolved that could tolerate the "poison". Later, about 2 billion years ago, other bacteria emerged that could actually use the oxygen. These bacteria ultimately went on to become animals, while the photosynthesizing bacteria responsible for the crisis became plants.

Oxygen continued to accumulate until about 1.5 billion years ago, when it reached a concentration of 21 percent, the level which, as we saw in Chapter 2, happens to be the optimal balance between metabolic efficiency and fire risk. Thereafter it abruptly stopped increasing and has remained stable ever since.

FROM CELL TO ORGANISM

Once the oxygen concentration had stabilized at this critical level, there came a series of important steps forward in the evolutionary process. Some simple cells began to be integrated within other simple cells, giving birth to more complex cells. These new cells were the first to possess a well-defined nucleus, within which the genetic material was encapsulated. The development of a nucleus made it possible for two cells to come together and produce offspring containing a combination of their genetic material; that is, sexual reproduction became possible. This opened greater opportunities for success and failure (as far as evolution is concerned, one success is worth a million failures) and allowed new adaptations to spread more quickly through a population, thus speeding up the rate of evolution.

As a greater variety of cells evolved, some cells appeared that were able to feed off other life-forms. (Until now, cells had consumed gases, minerals, organic molecules, and light energy.) With this development, cells no longer had to build up all their complex macromolecules from scratch but could take in many of them already formed, as amino acids, proteins, and vitamins. In effect, cells were now able to consume more highly organized matter.

The next major evolutionary development occurred around 1 billion years ago, as a result of a food crisis. Beyond a certain size, the cells could no longer take in enough nourishment to feed themselves. (As a cell grows, its volume increases faster than its surface area, and it is the surface area that limits the amount of food that can be absorbed.) Evolution's response was to limit the size of cells, and instead to produce larger systems by clumping together. So single cells began to gather themselves into small groups and colonies, giving rise to the first multicellular organisms: simple sponges and, later, jellyfish.

Within these communities it became more efficient for different cells to specialize in different functions. Some took on digestive tasks, some became a protective casing, and others conveyed messages to different parts of the organism. This conferred an added adaptability and stability on the organism, helping it to survive greater variations in the environmental conditions.

Another important characteristic of multicellular organisms was that individual cells could be replaced as they died, giving the organism as a whole the ability to live far longer than its constituents.

By about 600 million years ago, more complex multicellular organisms such as mollusks and simple worms began to develop. Over time, these multicellular organisms became progressively more organized. Different cells took on more specific functions and grouped themselves into specialized organs, leading to yet more complex organisms, some of them recognizable as the ancestors of modern plants and animals. About 450 million years ago, plants began to colonize the land, and animals joined them 50 million years later. (Plants were first since they could harvest the sun's energy directly. Once they started the food chain, animals followed.)

This is where the evolutionary tale with which most people are familiar comes in: the story of how these early organisms evolved through numerous stages into the millions of species of plants and animals living on the planet today. Since we are going to be concerned with the major leaps in evolution rather than its detailed development, we will not go into specifics here.

The most important general trend within this part of evolution was the development of the nervous system, permitting more rapid communication between different parts of the body. Within the vertebrates the main nerve fibers became enclosed in a protective tube (the spine), and the principal nerve centers at the top took on greater importance and became the first simple brain.

Within the last 50 million years, the brain has undergone an explosive growth, one of the most rapid and dramatic changes in the history of evolution. If we look at

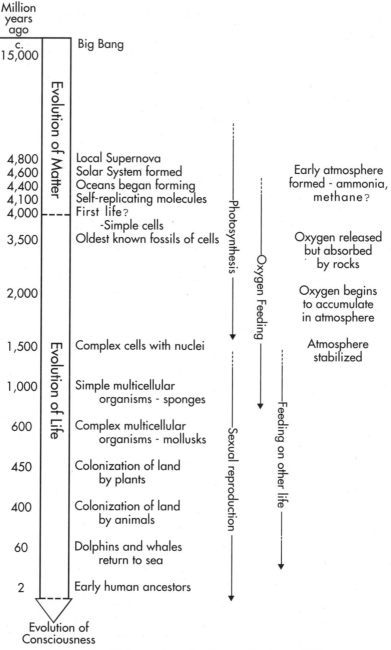

Figure 1. Major stages in the evolution of life.

the ratio of brain weight to body weight and start the scale with earthworms and insects as 1, then stenonychosaurus (one of the most intelligent dinosaurs, living about 75 million years ago) would be around the 20 mark, while human beings would be up at the 350 mark.

Even more significant, the cortex, the outer layer of the brain thought to be the seat of higher mental functions, has become relatively thicker and larger. The most developed cortices on this planet are to be found in human beings and in some of the cetaceans (dolphins and whales). (Whether dolphins and whales are more or less intelligent than humans is an open question; research in this area is still in its infancy. Indeed, the question is probably unanswerable in that it presumes some absolute definition of intelligence that is applicable to humans and dolphins alike.)

The brains of whales and dolphins appear to have stopped evolving 20 million years ago, long before the first humans appeared, suggesting that they may be perfectly adapted to their watery environment. The human brain, by contrast, is a relatively new evolutionary venture, having evolved only over the last 3 million years. It is almost certainly still evolving, though our human time frames may prevent us from being directly aware of this.

SELF-REFLECTIVE CONSCIOUSNESS

With the development of the large human brain and cortex, another major evolutionary leap occurred, as significant as the emergence of life itself. This was the emergence of

self-reflective consciousness. Humans are not only conscious; they are conscious of being conscious.

   Consciousness means different things to different people.
One dictionary definition is "knowing of external circumstances", which would imply that being asleep is a state of
unconsciousness. Yet we certainly have experiences when
we dream. Moreover, a person in a coma or under
anaesthesia may appear completely insensible to the people
around, yet upon awakening (or later, under hypnosis) may
accurately report conversations that occurred. Another use
of the word relates to the amount of attention put into an
action. If, while eating a meal, we are more engaged in the
conversation than the meal, we might be said to be eating
without consciousness of the process. Or, we may use the
word in the sense of intent or deliberation, as in making a
choice with full consciousness of its consequences. We
also talk of a person's social, political, or ecological consciousness, meaning that particular way he or she perceives
the world.

   The difficulty surrounding the meaning of the word
consciousness arises in part from the fact that in English
we have only one word to convey so many different mean-
ings. In Sanskrit, the ancient Indian language, there are
some twenty different words for consciousness, each with
its own specific meaning, some representing concepts with
which we in the West are barely familiar. For example, *chitta*
is the "mindstuff" or "experiencing medium" of the individual; *chit* is the "eternal consciousness" of which the
individual mindstuff is a manifestation; *turiya* is the experience of pure consciousness focused on an idea; *purusha*, the
essence of consciousness, is somewhat akin to the Holy Spirit.

Here I shall be using the word consciousness to mean the field within which all experience takes place. In this sense consciousness is a prerequisite for all experience whether we are awake, in a trance, dreaming, in a coma, or in any other state. We might draw an analogy with a film projected onto a screen. We may watch many different films on the same screen, but without the screen, we cannot see the film.

Consciousness in this sense is not restricted to human beings; any being that experiences has consciousness. Anyone who has spent time with other mammals, such as dogs, cats, or horses, has probably come to the conclusion that they are also conscious beings. They "know" what's going on. They are not automata. Birds, reptiles, and fish would also appear to have consciousness; maybe insects, snails, and worms do as well. According to some researchers, even plants appear to have some type of awareness.

An important characteristic attributed to conscious beings is the ability to form internal models of the world they experience; the greater the consciousness, the more complex the models. A worm probably has a relatively simple model of reality, whereas a dog's model would be considerably more complex. In human beings the nervous system has evolved to a point where our internal models of reality are so complex that they include the self—the "modeler"—in the model. This is the beginning of self-reflective consciousness. We not only experience the world around and within us, we also are aware of ourselves in that world and conscious that we are conscious.

The emergence of self-reflective consciousness is to some degree tied in with the development of language.

Language allowed humanity to communicate more widely and more fully. It also allowed us to focus attention on abstract and even hypothetical qualities of our experience, enabling us to separate the "experienced" from the "experiencer" (the self), a separation and objectification that, as we shall see in Chapter 12, has its drawbacks as well as its advantages.

The development of language led to the exchange of information between individuals. Thus a person could gain from the successes and failures of others, rather than having to learn everything from scratch. With drawing and writing came the ability to transfer information across time. This was as significant for the speeding of evolution as was the development of sexual reproduction, also an information transfer, in the single cell. The later invention of printing, and the more recent developments of photocopying, computing, and telecommunications, have likewise played a major part in accelerating the evolution of civilization.

So our brief review of evolution on this planet brings us to the present day. Suddenly, in a flash of evolutionary time, a new species has emerged: one that is aware of its own existence and one that holds awesome potential for consciously affecting itself and its environment.

This product of billions of years of evolution is truly something to marvel at. Here we are, each of us several septillion atoms arranged into an integrated system of some hundred trillion biological cells, experiencing the world around us and our thoughts, emotions, and desires. We can communicate these experiences to others in words and in a variety of other ways. We can imagine alternative futures and make choices to bring them about. We can even fantasize the impossible. Furthermore, we can look back and wonder at the whole evolutionary process, which has resulted step by step in me and in you, in farms, automobiles, and computers, in men walking on the moon, in the Taj Mahal, the *Emperor Concerto,* and the Theory of Relativity.

If anyone had been around four billion years ago, would they ever have guessed that the volcanic landscape, the primeval oceans, and the strange mixtures of gases in the atmosphere would steadily evolve into such improbable and complex beings as constitute humanity? If told, would they have believed it?

Could we now, if we were told what would happen in the next four billion years of evolution, believe it? Would the future seem as improbable to us as we seemed at the birth of the Earth? What unimaginable developments lie ahead, not only in thousands of millions of year's time, but in just one million years?

And what of the next few thousand years? The next hundred even? Where are we most likely to be headed? A look at the trends and patterns within the evolutionary process may give us some important clues to humanity's destination.

CHAPTER 5

HIDDEN ORDERS IN EVOLUTION

> Driven by the force of love, the fragments of the
> world seek each other that the world may come
> into being.
>
> *Teilhard de Chardin*

I f we stand back and consider the entire evolutionary process, a number of patterns seem to emerge. One of the first things we notice is that the universe today contains characteristics of which there were no traces in the beginning. Immediately after the Big Bang, there was only energy. Out of this developed a whole new order of existence: physical matter. For eons, this matter was inanimate, yet out of it emerged a new order: life. Life persisted and flourished, and from living organisms emerged another new order: self-reflective consciousness.

Each of these new orders of existence represented a major step forward in the evolutionary process, bringing with it novel properties and characteristics that could not have been predicted from the previous stage. Each new whole was more than the sum of its parts and not predictable in terms of its constituents.

We can see this happening with the progression from energy to matter, life, and consciousness. Mathematics, for example, which is sufficient to describe the electromagnetic radiation of energy, does not readily predict the behavior of molecules; this is the realm of chemistry. Chemistry likewise does not predict the principles that govern living organisms. And biology cannot readily describe conscious experience. Each of these new levels is a new phenomenon, a new emergent order of existence.

At the same time, the laws of the lower levels are still valid. Elementary particles in a cell continue to obey the laws of physics, atoms continue to obey the laws of chemistry, and macromolecules perform as expected by molecular biologists. Each new order subsumes all the previous orders; nothing is lost. Yet, something new is created, and the new phenomenon brings patterns of behavior that require a new level of understanding and explanation.

Western science sometimes finds it difficult to address the notion of emergent orders of existence. This is because one of the principal ways in which it has tried to understand the world is to break phenomena and processes down into smaller units, using what is called the reductionist approach. Although valuable in some areas, such as physical chemistry, engineering, and computer programming, it has the

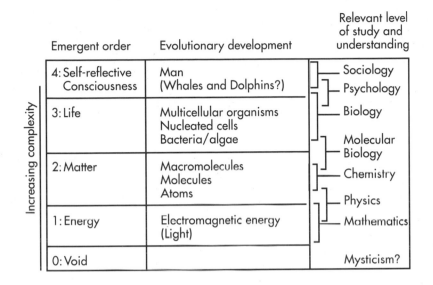

Table 2. Emergent orders of evolution showing fields of study relevant to the different stages.

drawback that emergent qualities of the whole system are usually lost or not dealt with.

The reductionist approach argues that consciousness can be explained in terms of neural events in the brain, and life in terms of organic chemistry. Taken to its logical conclusion, this argument ends up in a trap of its own making. Consciousness, it is said, is "nothing but" the cumulative effect of a complex interwoven web of ten billion nerve cells. A nerve cell is nothing but a huge conglomeration of macromolecules; a macromolecule is nothing but a few million atoms strung together; and an atom is nothing but a nucleus surrounded by a cloud of spinning electrons, which in turn are nothing but eigenvalues in a probability function called the wave equation. What is "an eigenvalue in a probability function"? Nothing but a model created by the conscious processes of the human mind in an attempt to give meaning to certain experimental results in physics. The argument has come full circle, for is not the human mind and its many faculties, including creativity and a sense of meaning, nothing but the workings of a few billion brain cells?

Consciousness *is* different from a collection of cells, just as life is different from a collection of atoms. Instead of arguing that consciousness is merely a by-product of brain activity, one could take the view that since consciousness evolves out of life, consciousness is already inherent within life in some potential latent form. Likewise, since life evolves from apparently inanimate matter, life is already inherent within matter in a latent form. Perhaps the potential for each new order is always present, awaiting the particular conditions that would allow it to become manifest.

What are these conditions? At least in part, the answer would seem to be a progressive increase in complexity.

EVOLVING COMPLEXITY

The word *complex* does not simply mean "having many parts". It also implies that the many parts are interrelated and interdependent (the Latin root of complex means interwoven or plaited). In contemporary systems theory, complexity is sometimes defined as a measure of the number of relationships among the different components of a system.

Complexity appears to have three basic characteristics:

Quantity/diversity: The system contains a large number of different elements.

Organization: The many components are organized into various interrelated structures.

Connectivity: The components are connected through physical links, energy interchanges, or some form of communication. Such connectivity maintains and creates relationships and organizes activity within the system.

In other words, for something to be called complex, it should be composed of a number of different elements, organized in some specific way and connected so as to interact with one another. To get a clearer idea of what this means, let us look at these characteristics at work in evolution.

Quantity/diversity. The bacterium *Escherichia coli*, which lives in the human intestine, is one of the simplest forms of life. Yet one such cell contains four DNA molecules, about 400,000 RNA molecules, about one million protein molecules, and some 500 million smaller organic molecules. Diversity is equally apparent in a complex organism, such as the human being, which contains many different types of cells (e.g., liver cells, brain cells, skin cells, blood cells, bone cells, and so on).

As far as the emergence of new evolutionary levels is concerned, a critical number of basic components seem to be required. The basic components of a living cell are atoms (stable units of matter). Within each cell of *Escherichia coli* there are about 40,000,000,000 atoms (written in mathematical shorthand as 4×10^{10}, where 10^{10} means ten raised to the tenth power, i.e., "1" followed by ten zeros). More complex cells such as a muscle cell may contain 10^{12} atoms, and some large amoeba may contain as many as 10^{15} atoms. In the other direction, however, we find very few cells containing less than 10^{10} atoms, and there are no known forms of life with less than 10^8 (i.e., a hundred million) atoms. In terms of sheer numbers, there would seem to be a threshold below which life does not readily emerge.

A similar threshold appears to exist for the emergence of self-reflective conscious forms of life. The average human brain contains about 10^{11} nerve cells, of which 10^{10} are in the cortex, the area associated with conscious thought processes. Brains with cortices containing 10^9 or fewer neurons, such as the brains of dogs, do not appear to show the phenomenon of self-reflective consciousness.

It appears that 10^{10} units are a sort of "magic number," the quantity of units needed for a new order of existence to emerge. If the quantity of elements collected together is significantly less than this number, there does not seem to be sufficient scope for the complex organization and interrelationships necessary for the emergence of a new level.

Organization. A macromolecule, such as a protein, is no mere random aggregation of atoms. Rather, the atoms are organized in a very specific structure, and just one atom out of place can radically change the characteristics and properties of the molecule. The millions of macromolecules that constitute a living cell are themselves organized into various organelles (the "organs" of the cell), which are in turn organized in specific ways, interact with each other at specific times for specific purposes, and generally synchronize their activities in ways that biologists are only just beginning to comprehend.

Similarly, our own bodies are highly organized collections of cells and organs. (The words *organism* and *organize* are derived from the same root.) Each of us contains some 10^{14} living cells, totaling around 5×10^{25} atoms, all organized in a very particular way so that the end result is a human being rather than a large bowl of soup.

Connectivity. Crucial to complexity is flow of matter, energy, and information among the many components and subsystems. The information exchange aspect is important to later discussions, so let us look briefly at how it manifests at various levels.

At the level of elementary physical matter, particles exchange rudimentary information about their charge, spin, and location through the basic physical forces (the gravitational force, the electromagnetic force, and the weak and strong nuclear forces). If, for example, two particles experience an electrostatic repulsion, they could be said to be receiving information that they are of opposite charges.

Further up the evolutionary scale, complex macromolecules exchange information about their shape and structure, as some molecules fit into the contours of other molecules like pieces in a jigsaw puzzle.

In simple living cells, information is transferred through the duplication process of asexual reproduction. The further evolutionary advance of sexual reproduction enabled the genes to transfer information from two parent cells to a new cell, thus increasing the quantity of information flowing from one generation to the next.

In simple organisms, information flows mainly with the aid of chemical messengers: hormones provide communication between one part of the system and another, and pheromones (chemicals released into the environment) convey information to other organisms (for example, the airborne sex attractants of moths and the scent trail of ants). Within more complex organisms, faster and more versatile forms of communication have been incorporated, employing the transmission of electrical impulses along nerves. Moving up to human society, we find the development of a variety of forms of interpersonal communication, such as speaking, writing, art, music, and, most recently, the emergence of telecommunications and computer networks.

In short, it would appear that one of the principal trends of evolution is a movement toward increasing complexity: individual units gather into larger and larger groups, which display increasing organization and structure as they expand, the many components interrelating in various ways.

Yet complexity appears to be more than just an evolutionary trend. It also seems to be the prerequisite for the emergence of new levels of evolution. Only when energy becomes organized in a particular way can the qualities of matter emerge and manifest themselves; only when many units of matter become collectively organized in a particular way can life emerge and manifest itself; and only when many living cells become collectively organized in a particular way does consciousness emerge and manifest itself.

ORDER VERSUS DISORDER

The evolutionary trend toward increasing complexity and organization might appear to be in opposition to a well-established law of physics, the second law of thermodynamics, which implies that the universe as a whole is moving steadily toward increasing disorder.

The second law of thermodynamics states that in any energy interaction there is a reduction in the "free energy"—

that is, the amount of energy available to perform useful work. For example, if you burn a piece of wood, energy is transformed from the energy of various chemical bonds into heat energy. Some of this energy could be harnessed to do useful work; it might heat the boiler of a steam engine, for instance. However, we can never again burn that piece of wood; the amount of free energy has decreased. Nor can the material be returned to its original state by mixing the ashes, smoke, and heat together.

Physicists measure the amount of energy in a system which is no longer available to do useful work in terms of a concept called entropy. When the free energy decreases, entropy is said to increase.

Entropy is also a measure of the amount of randomness in a system. When the entropy is at a minimum, the internal order of a system is at a maximum. As the entropy increases, the system becomes more disordered. Thus the second law of thermodynamics also implies that after an energy exchange, there is an increase in the disorder in the system.

As a simple example, imagine a drop of ink in a bowl of water. As the ink spreads out, its molecules go from a more concentrated and organized state to a more random distribution. To the non-physicist it might seem that the evenly distributed mix is the most orderly, but to a physicist or mathematician the most orderly state is the one in which the positions of the ink molecules are most easily defined, that is, when all the ink molecules are localized in a single drop. As the ink spreads and the molecules become more randomly distributed, the orderliness is said to decrease, and entropy to increase.

Elementary particles

combining to form

Atoms

combining to form

Molecules

combining to form

Macromolecules

combining to form

Simple cells

combining to form

Complex cells

combining to form

Tissues and organs

combining to form

Self-conscious organisms

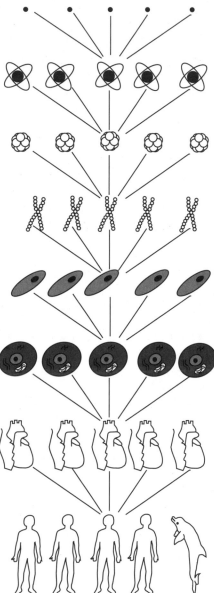

Figure 2. Evolution as a progressive collecting together of units into larger systems.

An important corollary of the second law is that such processes are irreversible. Systems do not spontaneously become more ordered; left on its own an ink solution does not return to being a concentrated drop. Since this law applies to all physical systems, the entropy of the universe as a whole must also be increasing. In other words, the physical universe is continually running down, moving toward more random, less orderly states.

Life, however, would appear to contradict this trend. Living systems display a great deal of order. Every living being, from the smallest bacterium to a blue whale, is a highly ordered collection of energy and matter. Over time, individual living systems not only retain a high degree of internal organization, they build up this order as they grow and develop. Life appears to move toward increasing order rather than disorder. But according to the second law of thermodynamics, a system such as your body should be gaining entropy, returning to a preblological soup. So does life somehow contravene a well-established and seemingly universal law of physics?

The answer is no, and the reason is that the second law only applies to *closed* systems, systems that are isolated from their environment so that there is no flow of matter or energy in or out of the system. (An example of a totally closed system would be a sealed container, perfectly insulated and impervious to vibration, sound, light, magnetic fields, X-rays, or any other form of energy transmission.)

Living systems, however, are *open* systems, continually exchanging energy and matter with their environment. When we consider an organism plus its entire environment as a single system, the second law of thermodynamics still holds, because we are now in effect considering a closed system. Bacteria living inside a closed container, for example, will show a decrease in entropy (i.e., an increase in their internal order), although the total entropy of the container and bacteria together will have increased.

Considered on its own, an organism effectively retains internal order at the expense of order in the environment. In the words of Erwin Schrödinger: "What an organism feeds upon is negative entropy; it continues to suck orderliness from its environment." Or, to put it another way, an organism exports entropy to its environment. This exportation may occur through the excretion of less-ordered material or through the emission of heat (heat energy consists of random molecular vibrations and is thus of high entropy). The net effect is that the resulting local decreases in entropy associated with a living system are paid for by larger increases in the entropy of the environment.

Nevertheless, even though living processes may not contradict the second law of thermodynamics, the question remains as to why an organism builds up and preserves a high degree of internal order. Why does a certain collection of atoms go against the trend of the rest of the universe? Indeed, if the entire evolutionary process can be seen as one of increasing organization, why does this happen within a universe that is, as a whole, running down toward disorder?

SELF-ORGANIZING SYSTEMS

For a long while there were no satisfactory scientific answers to these questions. In the 1970s, however, Ilya Prigogine, a Belgian physical chemist, working in Brussels and at the University of Texas, made a major breakthrough in understanding how order can arise from disorder—a breakthrough for which he won the 1977 Nobel Prize in chemistry. He noticed that there were a few physical and chemical systems that could build and maintain a high degree of order in their physical structure even though no such order was fed into them.

One particular chemical reaction, known as the Belousov-Zhabotinsky reaction, was the subject of considerable investigation by Prigogine and his colleagues, since it provided an excellent example of patterns of organization arising from a homogeneous mixture of substances. In this reaction, four chemicals (malonic acid, a sulfate of cerium, potassium bromate, and sulfuric acid) are mixed up in specific concentrations and left in a shallow dish to react. Within a few minutes concentric circles or spiraling waves are seen spreading out across the dish, and these patterns continue for several hours.

The chemical process displayed in this reaction is cross-catalytic, that is, the products of one stage act as catalysts for later stages. As a result, the reactions go through a series of repetitions that give rise to the distinctive patterns. The appearance of these ordered patterns represents a decrease in entropy within the dish, made possible by the exportation of entropy to the surroundings. Yet the net entropy of the whole system (the dish plus its environment) has increased, as would be predicted by the second law of thermodynamics.

Prigogine termed such self-ordering processes *dissipative structures,* since the entropy they produce is dissipated to the environment. A dissipative structure always produces entropy, but gets rid of this entropy through continuous interaction with the environment. As energy and matter are taken in, entropy (usually in the form of heat) and some end products are expelled, a process which might be termed the "metabolism" of the system.

Through their work, Prigogine and his colleagues found that three conditions are necessary before a dissipative structure can form:

Openness: Matter and energy must be able to flow between the system and its environment.

Far from equilibrium: Only if the system is far from the state of thermodynamic equilibrium can self-organization persist; near equilibrium the system behaves like any other physical system—there is increasing entropy.

Self-reinforcement: Certain elements of the system catalyze the production of new elements of the same kind, that is, the elements are self-reproducing.

If the energy or matter flowing through a dissipating system fluctuates, internal organization will be retained as long as the fluctuations remain within certain limits. The system can even suffer minor physical damage, yet "heal" itself through its self-organizing nature. If, however, the fluctuations increase beyond a certain limit, they will drive the system into instability.

Characteristic of these transitions is a period of considerable chaos within the system. This corresponds to a maximum flow of energy and matter through the system and maximum dissipation of entropy into the environment. As a result the system may collapse. But, alternatively, if the system survives this period, reorganization and a new level of stability can emerge. In other words, a dissipative system is capable of *evolving*.

DISSIPATIVE STRUCTURES IN EVOLUTION

The general behavior of dissipative structures seems very similar to that of living systems. Prigogine has shown that biological processes, far from being renegades in an otherwise disordering universe, are actually predictable by the principles of dissipative structures. He concluded: "Life no longer appears as an island of resistance against the Second Law of Thermodynamics. . . . It would appear now as a consequence of the general laws of physics . . . which permit the flow of energy and matter to build and maintain functional and structural order in open systems."

Biological systems have now become the prime focus of research in this field. Phenomena such as the growth of plants, the regeneration of limbs in simple organisms, the excitation pattern of nerve cells, and many biochemical processes can now be understood in terms of the principles found in dissipative structures. This theory has been applied to social groups such as bee swarms and slime molds, to human economic interactions, to human society, to ecosystems, and even to Gaia herself. The theory can also be applied to evolution in general. In his book, *The Self-Organizing Universe*, Eric Jantsch demonstrates that the trend of evolution toward increasing complexity can, at each stage, be understood as the effect of dissipative systems.

As mentioned above, extreme fluctuations within dissipative structures can lead to the emergence of new levels of organization. In evolutionary terms these fluctuations appear as periods of instability, or crises, in which organisms are forced either to adapt to the changed environment, perhaps moving on to higher levels of organization, or to be extinguished.

An early crisis, or fluctuation, in the evolution of life possibly occurred when the simple organic compounds on which the first primitive cells fed started running short. There was, in effect, a food crisis. The response was the evolution of photosynthesis, the ability to feed directly from sunlight.

Photosynthesis produced oxygen as a by-product, and 1.5 billion years later, as the oxygen began to build up in the atmosphere, there was another crisis, this time of pollution and poison. The response was the evolution of oxygen-breathing cells.

Later, as cells became more complex and grew in size, they could not absorb food fast enough to nourish themselves. This time the evolutionary response was to develop multicellular organisms.

Looking at humanity from the perspective of dissipative systems, we can see that the two principal characteristics of a major fluctuation seem to be present: increasing flow of energy and matter, combined with high entropy. We are now consuming energy and matter like never before, with all the ensuing problems of resource scarcity and depletion. At the same time the entropy produced by humanity has shot up, resulting in increasing disorder both within society and the environment.

Humanity appears to be rapidly approaching the breaking point. And there are two possible outcomes: breakdown or breakthrough. If we cannot adapt to the pressures being brought to bear, human society may well collapse. If we can adapt, we may move on to a new level. One thing seems clear: the pace of change is increasing, and whichever route we take, major changes are not far away.

CHAPTER 6

THE INCREASING
TEMPO OF EVOLUTION

"A slow sort of country!" said the Queen. "Now,
here, you see, it takes all the running you can
do, to keep in the same place. If you want to get
somewhere else, you must run at least twice as
fast as that!"
Alice Through the Looking Glass,
Lewis Carroll

It is commonplace today to speak of the pace of life speeding up and look back with nostalgia at the more leisurely existence of our grandparents' time. But this speeding up is not new; it has been going on for 15 billion years, since the dawn of creation.

In evolution each new development was able to draw upon what had already been accomplished. (The evolution of complex macromolecules, for example, utilized the properties and characteristics of less complex molecules such as amino acids, aldehydes, and water.) Each new phenomenon became another platform that evolution could use in its movement toward yet greater complexity—the broader the platform, the greater the rate of development. This has produced an accelerating pattern of growth.

As a result of this natural tendency to accelerate, the major developments in evolution have not occurred at regular intervals; rather, the intervals have been shortening. When we talk in terms of billions of years, however, it may sometimes be difficult to see this happening. To get a more tangible image, compress these 15 billion years into a film a year long—the ultimate epic.

The Big Bang, with which the film opens, is over in a hundred-millionth of a second. The universe cools rapidly, and within about twenty-five minutes stable atoms have formed. No more significant changes happen during the rest of the first day, nor for the rest of January; the only thing there is to view is an expanding cloud of gas. Around February and March the gas clouds begin slowly condensing into clusters of galaxies and stars. As the weeks and months pass by, stars occasionally explode in supernovae, new stars condensing from the debris. Our own sun and solar system are eventually formed in early September— after eight months of film.

Once the Earth has been formed, things move a little faster as complex molecules start to take shape. Within two weeks, by the beginning of October, simple algae and bacteria appear. Then comes a relative lull while bacteria slowly evolve, developing photosynthesis a week later, with the consequent buildup of an oxygen atmosphere after five more weeks, in early November. Within another week, complex cells with well-defined nuclei evolve, making sexual reproduction possible, and with this stage accomplished, evolution accelerates again. It is now late November, and the major part of the film is over. The evolution of life, however, has only just begun.

The first simple multicellular organisms appear around early December, and the first vertebrates crawl out of the sea onto land a week or so later. Dinosaurs rule the land for most of the last week of the film, from Christmas to midday on December 30th—a long and noble reign!

Our early apelike ancestors make their debut around the middle of the last day, but not until eleven o'clock in the evening do they walk upright.

Now, after 365 days and nights of film, we come to some of the most fascinating developments. Human language begins to develop one and a half minutes before midnight. In the last half minute farming begins. Buddha achieves enlightenment five and a half seconds before the end, and Christ appears a second later. The Industrial Revolution begins in the last half second, and World War II occurs less than a tenth of a second before midnight.

We are down to the last frame now, the last inch of a 100,000 miles of film. The rest of modern history happens in a flash, not much longer than the flash with which the film started. Moreover, evolution is continuing to accelerate, and this rapid acceleration shows no signs of abating. Wherever we are going, we are going there fast.

EVOLUTIONARY LEAPS

If we plot the evolutionary changes we have just reviewed, we would see that, within the acceleration, periods of rapid growth follow periods of much slower development. Acceleration has not occurred smoothly; rather, it appears to have happened in a series of sudden steps.

Let us consider, for instance, the process that occurred after the sudden formation of stable atoms of hydrogen, some 70,000 years after the Big Bang. Over billions of years, these atoms slowly evolved into other simple elements. The greater the variety of atoms that were created, the greater the potential for more atoms to form. Thus, over time, this platform-building process accelerated until a stage was reached where most of the heavier elements were formed quite suddenly, in a period of some fifteen minutes, in the heart of exploding stars.

Another series of accelerations occurred in the transition from matter to life. Before the development of stars with planetary systems, the only mechanisms available to evolution were at the atomic and subatomic levels. Once the cooler conditions necessary for the formation of more complex molecules existed, evolution had another foothold on which to build and could go much faster. The more complex the molecules it produced, the greater scope there was for further evolution. So the process speeded up until simple bacteria emerged.

This occurred relatively early in Earth's history, some four billion years ago. At this stage evolution stepped onto a new platform, the platform of life. But life at this time was still very simple and offered little variety, and the process slowed down again. It took between ten and twenty times as long for cells with a simple nucleus to emerge from bacteria as it did for bacteria to emerge from the prebiotic soup. But once nucleated cells appeared, they were capable of sexual reproduction, which in turn led to greater variation and adaptability. With the continued creation of more and more complex forms, the platform of life expanded, and evolution moved on faster and faster.

The evolution of the many different species of animals was probably also an intermittent process. The classical view of biological evolution, based on Darwin's theories, held that a species evolved slowly through a long series of

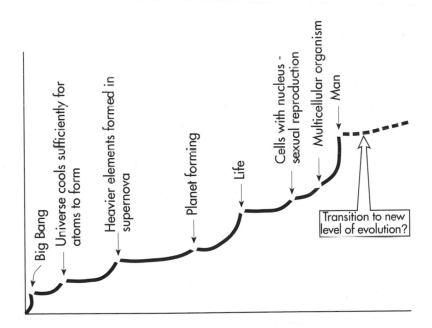

Figure 3. Evolution as a series of sudden transitions.

minor changes, and over millions of years this process led to the emergence of completely new species. While most of the general principles of Darwinian evolution are accepted by the vast majority of scientists, certain aspects of his theory have recently been called into question. Rather than finding fossils that represent a smooth progression from one species to another, we find a large number of fossils for one species, plus a large number for the species that it appears to have evolved into, with very little in between. Some evolutionary theorists, such as Stephen Jay Gould, now believe that individual species have enjoyed long periods of stability followed by periods of rapid evolution, with these relatively sudden changes probably occurring in response to major environmental changes. Just how quickly these evolutionary leaps might have taken place is still being debated. It is possible that they happened in 50,000 years or so, which in evolutionary terms is quick compared with ten million years, and they might, in the right circumstances, have happened in only a thousand years. In some instances developments have been observed to take place even faster; some present-day species of birds and moths have been observed undergoing major changes in just one generation.

With the appearance of humanity, evolution moved from the biological level to a new level: self-reflective consciousness. We are, it is almost certainly true, still evolving as a species, but this process, rapid as it may be from an evolutionary perspective, is occurring relatively slowly as far as human time scales are concerned. As far as we can tell, we are physiologically very similar to human beings ten thousand years ago. What is evolving, and evolving very rapidly, is the human mind and the ways in which we apply it.

Self-reflective consciousness brought with it the ability to direct our own destiny. Humanity is not bound to a long, slow adaptation process through trial and error; rather, we can anticipate the results of our actions and consciously choose those that are most likely to take us where we want to go—as individuals and as a species. As a result, human evolution has taken a huge leap forward, so much so that we now appear to be in the midst of an unprecedented period of extremely rapid development.

ACCELERATION TODAY

The rate of change in many areas of activity is now so fast that it is hard to imagine where we will be in fifty years' time, let alone a hundred or thousand years from now. Never before has a product of evolution participated so actively in accelerating the evolutionary process. Here are just a few examples:

Biology. Biology developed slowly until the seventeenth century, when the invention of the microscope led to the discovery of cells. Further advances included the classification of species, the discovery of viruses, and an understanding of genetic principles, all of which pushed biology ahead. In the twentieth century, the science accelerated further through the development of biochemistry, more precise instruments, electron microscopy, and computer processing. Today we are even mapping the detailed molecular structure of a gene.

Recently, human beings have become more than just

passive observers of the living world. Within the last decades biologists have learned how to modify the genes in a cell, opening the door to the creation of completely new species. Now new life-forms can be designed consciously and created rapidly.

From an evolutionary perspective, this is an extremely significant event. The only innovation that comparably expanded life's ability to diversify itself was the development of sexual reproduction two billion years ago. Yet even this capacity took a billion years to evolve; human science has achieved a comparable step in just a few hundred.

Atomic Physics. In 1808, the British chemist John Dalton discovered that different elements have different atomic weights. After the discovery of electrons in 1897, it was realized that atoms were not the smallest units but were comprised of yet smaller particles. By the 1930s physicists had settled on a standard atomic model: a nucleus, consisting of protons and neutrons, with electrons in discrete orbits around it. This marked the birth of atomic physics.

With the advent of particle accelerators, scientists once again became more than just passive observers. They were now able to change some elements into others, or even create completely new elements, by bombarding the nucleus with atomic particles and thereby changing its structure.

The evolutionary significance of this development can be more fully grasped when we realize that the last time new elements were synthesized was in a supernova explosion prior to our Sun's formation. In other words, humanity is initiating a process that has not occurred in this part of the universe for over five billion years.

Energy Sources. On Earth the major conversion of the sun's energy occurs through photosynthesis of light by plants. The energy in wood, peat, coal, and oil was all initially produced by photosynthesis, though in some cases millions of years ago. In the last hundred years, however, we have created a fundamentally new way of directly harnessing the sun's energy, the solar cell. This invention represents an evolutionary development as significant as that of photosynthesis 3.5 billion years ago.

Mobility. Over the millennia human travel has progressed from walking to horseback, to boats, to trains and cars, to supersonic jets, and to space rockets travelling at 25,000 miles per hour. At each stage there has been a leap in speed and distance traveled, and each increase has been greater than the one before. Moreover, the intervals between each new development have been rapidly shortening. We now stand on the threshold of the colonization of space, a development as significant as the colonization of land by the first amphibians 1,000 million years ago.

Communication. Humanity's ability to transfer information has progressed from speech and drawing, to writing, to printing, to telegraph, to telephone, to radio, to television, to photocopying, to computers, to global telecommunication networks, increasing significantly the quantity, quality, and availability of information. The combined effect of these developments has been the progressive linking of humanity, a trend which, as we shall see later, seems to be crucially important for our continued evolution, and whose evolutionary parallel can be found in the emergence of the first multicellular organisms one billion years ago.

Were only one of these developments occurring today, we would be living in an evolutionarily important time. But the fact that these momentous changes are occurring simultaneously suggests that we are in the midst of a phase that has no evolutionary precedent.

Moreover, these developments are cross-catalytic: progress in one field accelerates progress in another. Molecular biology, for example, has been accelerated by microscopy, computer analysis, chemical theory, chromatography, and microanalysis; the resultant advances in molecular biology have in turn fed back into such areas as medicine, agriculture, chemistry, industry, and technology. This speeding up, through the simultaneous convergence of so many different growths, is itself something that has happened only rarely in the history of evolution and never before as rapidly or with so many widespread and diverse implications.

It certainly seems as if we who are alive today are at a unique point in evolution. As John Platt, a systems theorist long fascinated by the acceleration of evolution, wrote in *The Futurist:*

> Jumps by so many orders of magnitude, in so many areas, with this unprecedented coincidence of several jumps at the same time, and these unique disturbances of the planet, surely indicate that we are not passing through a smooth cyclical or acceleration process similar to those in the historical past. Anyone who is willing to admit that there

have been sudden jumps in evolution or human history, such as the invention of agriculture or the Industrial Revolution, must conclude from this evidence that we are passing through another such jump far more concentrated and more intense than these, and of far greater evolutionary importance.

If this is so, if the rapid acceleration so characteristic of today is heading us toward an evolutionary leap, what lies beyond? Could we be on the threshold of a leap as significant as the evolution of life from inanimate matter?

CHAPTER 7

GROWING NUMBERS

> In today's world all curves are exponential. It is
> only in mathematics that exponential curves
> grow to infinity. In real life they either break
> down catastrophically or they saturate gently.
>
> *Denis Gabor*

From the birth of the universe to the present time,
evolution has inexorably pushed toward greater and
greater levels of complexity: increasing diversity, organization, and connectivity. Out of this growing complexity, new
orders of evolution have emerged. There is no logical reason to suppose that this trend should stop now. On the
contrary, it shows every sign of continuing. The three principal aspects of complexity once again appear to be reaching
the point where a new order of existence could emerge,

and the arena for this next evolutionary breakthrough could very well be humanity itself.

For us to assess the level of complexity in society today, let us look first at diversity. In evolutionary terms, diversity has two major components. The first is variety, the development of a wide range of types within the group. Clearly this has happened within humanity. No matter how the human species is subdivided—by nationality, race, body type, or belief system—there is no shortage of variety.

The second aspect of diversity is increasing numbers. The human population has been rapidly expanding, and many see this as a negative trend. But from an evolutionary perspective, increasing numbers are vital, as they contribute to the complexity upon which evolution builds.

The growth of nearly all populations, whether they be bacteria in a dish, cells in an embryo, or rabbits in Australia, initially follows a pattern of rapidly increasing growth typified by what is called the exponential curve. Since the nature of this curve is important for the discussions that follow, let us take a look at some of its properties.

In exponential growth, the rate of growth is directly proportional to the current size. This means that the bigger something is, the faster it grows. Population is a classic example. The rate of growth of a population depends upon the number of people already living, and so an expanding population— provided there are no sudden decreases caused by war, disease, famine, and so forth—tends to grow more and more rapidly. Another example of exponential growth occurs when money is invested at compound interest. The interest is calculated on the initial capital plus all interest accrued so far; more and more interest is added each year, giving rise to the typical exponential curve shown in Figure 4.

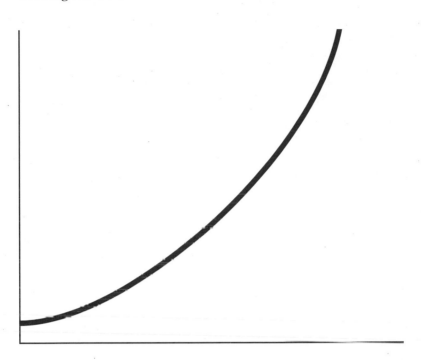

Figure 4. An exponential curve, typifying the growth of a population, money invested at compound interest, or any other growth in which the rate of increase is directly proportional to the current size.

An important aspect of the curve should be noted. As the curve gets steeper and steeper, it can look as if it would eventually be going up vertically. This never actually happens; if it did it would imply that at a certain time the population (or whatever) would have become infinitely large.

Every exponential curve, because it grows at a constant percentage rate, has its own particular "doubling time". This is the time it takes for the population (or whatever is being measured) to double its size. A simple mathematical relationship exists between the percentage growth rate and the doubling time: doubling time equals 70 divided by growth rate (69.31 divided by growth rate, to be a little more precise). Thus, if the population were growing at the rate of two percent per year, it would have a doubling time of thirty-five years. (This relationship will be useful later when we come to consider the implications of the growth rates of various aspects of society.)

The exponential curve is, of course, a mathematical model, and natural growths seldom follow this pattern exactly. For example, the growth of human population has not followed a true exponential curve. Over the centuries the doubling time has steadily shortened. In the year 1000 A.D. the world population was around 340 million, with a doubling time of about five hundred years. By the seventeenth century, the doubling time had dropped to three hundred years; in 1800 it was down to one hundred years; in 1940 it was about fifty years; and by the 1960s it was doubling every thirty-five years.

This type of growth, increasing more rapidly than even an exponential growth, is called "superexponential". Such curves occur whenever the rate of growth not only depends on the current size of the population but also builds on what already has been achieved in the past. (If, for example, a bank were to add up the sums that appeared on each of your annual statements and pay you interest on that total rather than your current statement, you would have a superexponentially increasing account and would soon be very rich indeed.) In the case of the human population, this superexponential growth is a direct consequence of the development of language, writing, printing, and communication systems, which have brought with them the

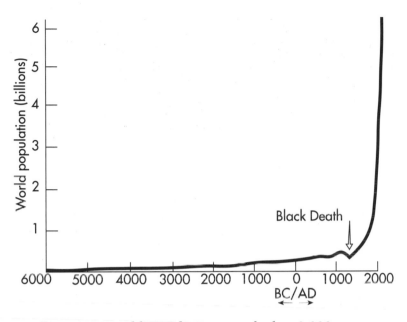

Figure 5. World population over the last 8,000 years.

ability to pool the knowledge acquired over time. This has led to better health care, increased production, higher standards of living, and more efficient land use—factors that have enabled the population to grow faster and faster.

In practice, no exponential growth or any superexponential growth can go on increasing forever. Eventually it will reach limits imposed by the physical environment. Bacteria in a dish, doubling every few hours, cannot do more than fill the dish. Humanity cannot, at present, do more than fill the planet. At some point a growing population will start to feel the environment's inability to support ever-increasing numbers—usually when it is about halfway to the maximum. The growth rate will then begin to slow down, and the curve will start bending over in the opposite direction, producing an S-shaped curve (see Figure 6).

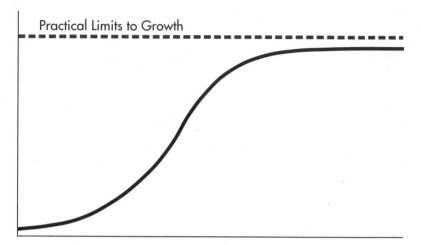

Figure 6. As an exponentially growing population begins to approach the limits imposed by its environment, it changes into an S-curve.

In the case of bacteria in a dish, this slowing of growth is brought about by such forces as lack of food and lack of space—factors that are beyond its control. In the case of the future growth of human population, we might expect similar forms of "natural" control, such as disease, famine, or even wars resulting from conflicts over diminishing food, resources, water, and energy supplies. Unlike bacteria, however, humanity has both consciousness and graph paper. We can anticipate the future and apply human decision-making to population control, giving us the possibility of preempting the various means of natural control and avoiding apocalypse.

Recent data on human population suggest that its growth has already begun to slow. The most accurate figures come from the developed nations, and in nearly all of these, fertility (defined as the average number of children born per woman) is steadily decreasing. Several European countries have already reached zero population growth, and the U.S.A. is not far behind, with the fertilities below strict replacement level. (The fact that fertility may have dropped below replacement level does not necessarily mean that the population immediately stops growing. It will often continue increasing for as much as twenty years because the number of potential parents may still be growing as a result of earlier birth rates.) In China, with a quarter of the world's population, there has for more than thirty years been a policy of one child per family. As a result reproduction there has likewise dropped below replacement level, and China hopes to reach zero growth soon after the year 2000.

Data for the world as a whole show a similar slowing in annual growth rates. It reached a peak of 2 percent in the early sixties—the turning point on the population S-curve. By 1970 it had dropped to 1.9 percent, and by 1980 to 1.7 percent. In the 1960s the average global fertility rate was 6 children per female. Today it is 3.5.

What will happen if these trends continue? The general consensus is that world population will be more than 6 billion by 2000 A.D., and will probably stabilize somewhere between 10 and 12 billion by the end of the twenty-first century.

The possibility that the population may stabilize around 10^{10} is of interest. As we have already seen, this figure may represent the approximate number of elements needed for a new level of evolution to emerge. (There are approximately this number of atoms in a simple living cell, and approximately the same number of cells in the cortex of the human brain.) If the same pattern occurs at higher

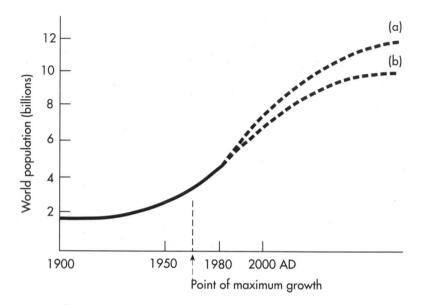

Figure 7. Predictions of future growth of world population by: (a) United Nations, (b) World Bank, showing slowing of growth rate and eventual stabilization between 10 and 12 billion.

levels of integration, then humanity may be reaching the size at which there are sufficient numbers of self-reflective conscious beings on the planet for the next level to emerge.

However, we may not have to wait for the end of the twenty-first century to see this possibility. The number 10^{10} is not an exact requirement; rather, it refers to what mathematicians call an order of magnitude (numbers that do not differ by more than a factor of ten, i.e. have the same number of digits). Thus the current (late 1994) population of 5.6 billion (5.6×10^9) is of the same order of magnitude as 10 billion, and may already be well within the range necessary for the emergence of a new level of evolution.

The Organized Organism

Numbers alone are not enough to bring about a major evolutionary leap. Ten billion atoms put together on a pinpoint do not make a living cell, nor do 10 billion neurons in a glass jar constitute a conscious brain. The elements need to be integrated into a cohesive structure and their interaction needs to be organized.

The first step toward this organization is usually *clumping*, the trend toward groupings of components. Considering society, we can trace steady movement from small groups of nomadic hunter-gatherers to farming communities, from tribal villages and hereditary clans to small countries and states, and from nations to larger groups such as the United States, the British Commonwealth, and the European Community, which transcend geographic and racial boundaries.

As the groups have become larger and more integrated, so have they become more organized. Just as a cell has its organelles and the body its organs, so society has its organization and structure. Rather than everyone doing much the same tasks, as in primitive hunter-gatherer societies, modern societies are characterized by a high degree of specialization.

Today almost everybody is a specialist, and the resulting interdependence and interaction of human society have given rise to a highly complex social structure. Just to drive to the store for a bottle of orange juice depends upon an interconnected worldwide network of people working in such diverse places as a rubber farm, an oil field, a refinery, a steel mill, a copper mine, an automobile manufacturing plant, an orange orchard, a glass company, and various import, export, and distribution companies, to mention just a few.

The increasing organization in society is not only found at the physical level. With the evolution of human beings there emerged self-reflective consciousness and the ability to think about the world we inhabit. This opened up the possibility of evolution at the mental level, and we can find the trend toward greater organization manifesting within us in various ways.

Intelligence itself is an organizing principle within human consciousness. In its most general sense, intelligence can be thought of as the ability to abstract order from raw sensory data, organize our perceptions into meaningful wholes, form relationships between them (concepts, expectations, hypotheses, etc.), and thereby organize action in a purposeful way.

The many facets of human knowledge can also be considered as ways of organizing our experiences of the world. Each individual scientific discipline represents a particular way of looking for underlying rules and laws revealing the order of the world we live in. Art, likewise, attempts to bring to human consciousness hidden orders of creation. In these, and many other ways, human beings are continually discovering new relationships, increasingly organizing their information about the world.

Human society has taken this one stage further. We not only organize information within ourselves, we can share that information with others. Through a variety of means of communication we are beginning to link at a level of consciousness, thereby enhancing the third crucial aspect of complexity—connectivity.

CHAPTER 8

TOWARDS A GLOBAL BRAIN

> Remember that you are at an exceptional hour
> in a unique epoch, that you have this great
> happiness, this invaluable privilege,
> of being present at the birth of a new world.
> *The Mother, Sri Aurobindo Ashram*

To understand fully the significance of today's developments in the area of communications, we need to go back in time to consider the social changes that have occurred over the last two hundred years. In this short period, the thrust of human activity has altered significantly.

Prior to the eighteenth century, the majority of the population (about 90 percent) was employed in the production of food—agriculture and fishing, for instance—and its distribution. This percentage had stayed constant for hundreds of years, the actual number increasing at about the same rate as the population itself. In the early 1800s its doubling time was around 45 years. With the advent of the Industrial Revolution, however, the increasing application of technology to farming led to a slowing in the growth rate of agricultural employment, and the curve began to bend over in the characteristic S-shape.

From the beginning of the nineteenth century the more developed nations have shown a steady increase in the number of people employed in industry and manufacturing—a shift away from the processing of food towards the processing of minerals and energy. Employment statistics for the U.S.A. show that the growth of industrial employment was considerably faster than that of agricultural employment, doubling about once every 16 years, and by 1900 equal numbers of people (about 38 percent) were employed in each sector. In terms of employment, therefore, this date could be taken to mark the beginning of the Industrial Age in the U.S.A.

For the next seventy years, industry was the dominant activity in the U.S.A. Over the last few decades, however, the invention of computers and the consequent increase in information-processing capacities has brought about another shift. The steady application of technology and automation to industry caused the rate of growth of industrial employment to slow, giving rise once again to an S-curve. At the same time the number of people employed in information processing in its various forms—printing, publishing, accounting, banking, journalism, TV, radio, and telecommunications, as well as computing and its many ancillary occupations—has been growing at an exponential rate. Its doubling time may now be as short as six years.

By the mid-1970s the number of people in the U.S.A. engaged in the processing of information had caught up with those engaged in industry—the processing of energy and matter. From that time on, information processing became our dominant activity. We had entered the "Information Age".

Although these developments refer specifically to the U.S.A., parallel changes can be found in most of the more developed nations. The less developed nations show simi-

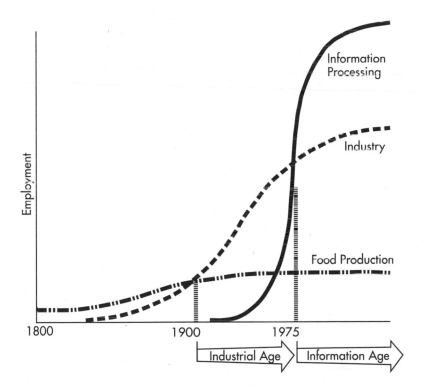

Figure 8. Changes in the number of people involved in different categories of human activity: food production, industry, and information processing.

lar tendencies, but they lag behind the more developed ones to varying degrees. These lags, however, will almost certainly decrease as time goes on.

While a developing country may be fifty years behind the West in reaching the stage at which industrial activity becomes dominant, it may only be ten years behind when it makes the transition to an information-dominant society. Japan is an example of a country which, despite a late start, has quite definitely caught up with the West. South Korea moved from the Agricultural Age to the Information Age in only fourteen years. Many of the Middle East, oil-rich nations, such as Kuwait and Saudi Arabia, are also making rapid strides. China, although still predominantly agricultural, may spend only a short time in the Industrial Age before shifting to an information society. And it may well be that other countries will skip the Industrial Age entirely—at least as far as majority employment is concerned.

LANGUAGE LINKS

As more and more nations of the world move into the Information Age, the technology of communications and information processing will dramatically affect the human race, as we become increasingly integrated through the burgeoning network of electronic synapses.

If we look back over human history, we can see that this trend toward a progressive linking of humanity seems to have been going on for millennia. The sudden surge of information technology in the present day can be seen as the fruit of millions of years of human effort.

The first major step toward interconnection came with the development of verbal language. This led to a profound and fundamental change in the way we gained knowledge about the world. All other creatures (with the possible exception of whales and dolphins) learn primarily from their own experience of life. A dog learns through what happens to it in its own life, it does not benefit significantly from the experiences of other dogs elsewhere in the world. But with the advent of symbolic language human beings could begin to share experiences and so learn not only from their own lives but also from others'.

This was a major evolutionary leap, as significant perhaps as the appearance of sexual reproduction two billion years ago. Two cells could come together and through the exchange of genetic information share their hereditary databanks—a breakthrough which, as we have seen, allowed new species to emerge thousands of times faster. Similarly, through language, human beings can exchange their own experiences and learnings, and the result has been a similar leap in the rate of evolution.

Language allowed us to shift from biological evolution to the much faster evolution of mind. Not only did our ability to learn from each other enhance our individual lives, it also led us into the whole new arena of group evolution. We became a collective learning system, building a collective body of knowledge that far exceeded the experience of any individual, but which any individual could, in principle, access. Through language we made the step from isolated organisms to a collective organism—much as a billion years ago single cells came together to make the first multicellular creatures.

The rate of growth of this collective learning system was greatly enhanced by a series of breakthroughs in information technology. Today we tend to think of information technology in terms of computers and telecommunications, but these are themselves the consequence of a whole series of breakthroughs in information technologies dating back to the dawn of civilization.

The first great breakthrough was the invention of writing, some ten thousand years ago. Before writing, knowledge was handed down primarily by word of mouth, a process that was very open to distortions, omissions, and misunderstandings. Writing made it possible to record our personal and cultural histories in a more reliable form and hand them down to future generations. The technological breakthrough of paper made records much easier to transport. We could share our knowledge with people in distant lands, linking human communities together.

The advent of the printing press in the fifteenth century further increased humanity's ability to disseminate written information. No longer did each copy of a manuscript have to be reproduced by hand—a process that was both slow and prone to error—thousands could be manufactured from the same original, virtually simultaneously. In the first fifty years after the invention of printing, around 80 million books were produced. The philosophies of the Greeks and Romans were distributed, the Bible became widely accessible, and through various "how to" books the skills of many crafts were made more widely available, paving the way for the Renaissance.

The next major breakthrough occurred in the mid-nineteenth century. This was the development of electrical communication in the form of the telegraph, and later the telephone. The time taken to transmit a message across the world suddenly dropped from days or weeks to minutes and then fractions of a second.

Fifty years later another breakthrough occurred through the use of radio waves as the transmission medium. This freed people from the need to be physically linked by cable and simultaneously made it possible to transmit a message to large numbers of people, that is, to broadcast information. Since then, radio and its offshoot, television, which literally gave us the ability to "see at a distance", have expanded rapidly, enabling the individual to be an eyewitness to events happening around the world.

At the same time that radio and television were spreading across the planet, another equally important development in information technology was occurring: electronic computers.

THE DIGITAL REVOLUTION

The first computer was built during World War II, to help the intelligence services in the complex task of breaking sophisticated codes. At the same time there arose an increasing need to be able to perform the complex calculations associated with technical design much more rapidly than could be done by paper, pencil, and adding machine. To fulfill these needs technicians designed electronic calculators—often the size of a room—and these gave birth to early electronic computers in the 1950s. Although cumbersome and slow by today's standards, these devices nevertheless represented a huge leap forward in terms of information processing power. During the 1960s and 1970s, dramatic strides were made in the computer's processing capacity and speed. Simultaneously the physical size of computers shrank remarkably.

The microprocessor, or "chip" as it is commonly called, represented a major revolution in computing technology. Less than a quarter of an inch in size, the average chip of 1990 contained more computing power than all the computers of 1950 put together, and this capacity has been doubling every year. In addition to the many advantages of its minute size, the chip's energy consumption is astoundingly low. The average computer of 1970 used more energy than 5,000 pocket calculators of similar computing capacity a mere ten years later. The information/energy ratio has been steadily increasing and is now rocketing. We are able to do more and more with less and less.

At the same time the cost of information processing has been falling dramatically. Computing power is often measured in millions of instructions per second (MIPS). The first transistorized computers of the 1950s (IBM's 7090, for example) managed to reach about 1 MIPS, and cost a million dollars. When the early integrated circuit computers of the late sixties, such as DEC's PDP 10, reached 10 MIPS, the price per MIPS had fallen to $100,000. The Apple II, which heralded the personal computer revolution in the mid-1970s, brought the cost down to below ten thousand dollars per MIPS. By 1990 the average PC cost around $1,000 per MIP, while supercomputers like the Cray 3, operating at 100,000 MIPS cost about $10 million, or $100 per MIPS. In 1994 personal computing power was also approaching $100 per MIPS. And it will continue falling in the future. By the year 2000 you will probably be able to buy the equivalent computing power of an IBM 7090 for ten dollars or less.

Whereas in 1970 computers were used almost solely by large institutions such as governments and corporations, the microprocessor—a microchip that is a computer in itself—has made it possible for the technology of computers and data processing to be available, potentially, to anyone on the planet without draining the planet of its vital energy resources. If comparable changes had been made in various aspects of the automobile over the last twenty years, a Rolls Royce would now cost fifty cents. It would be less than a tenth of an inch long, have a gasoline consumption of ten million miles per gallon, cruise at a hundred thousand miles per hour, and never need servicing! These tiny chariots would also be so commonplace as to be unremarkable. By the early 1990s there were more than 100 million personal computers in the world, and they were rolling off production lines at the rate of more than 100,000 per day.

THE NET

Another significant development has been the direct linking of computers. The first computers were independent units, interacting only with their human operators (there were no operating systems in those days). By the late 1960s, however, computers were able to communicate directly with each other. In 1969 the U.S. Advanced Research Projects Agency (ARPA) began an experiment to link computers across long distances so that they could exchange files and run programs on each other. The network grew slowly at first, but then more rapidly. Over the next decade a new computer was added to ARPAnet once every 20 days on average.

By the mid-1970s other networks had emerged, and began to interlink with ARPAnet. This new network of networks became known as the "internetwork"—and soon just "Internet". The net, as it is also sometimes called, continued to expand rapidly as many other host computers from around the world connected into it (see Figure 9). By 1994 Internet had grown into a massive web of networks with more than two million host computers and an estimated forty million users—and its size was doubling every year.

The number of bulletin boards, "places" on the network where people can access data on specialized subjects, have discussions, and meet others of like interests, has likewise exploded. In 1987 there were 6,000 bulletin boards (or BBSs). By 1994 there were close to 60,000, and the number was doubling every eighteen months.

Over the same period commercial services such as Compuserve, America Online, and Prodigy have also grown rapidly, bringing thousands of databases, computer shopping, newspapers, magazines, educational courses, airline schedules and e-mail directly into millions of homes.

Such prodigious rates of growth cannot continue far into the future. If Internet were to continue doubling every year, it would reach more than a billion people by 1999—which is more than the probable number of people able to afford the luxury of a personal computer and an

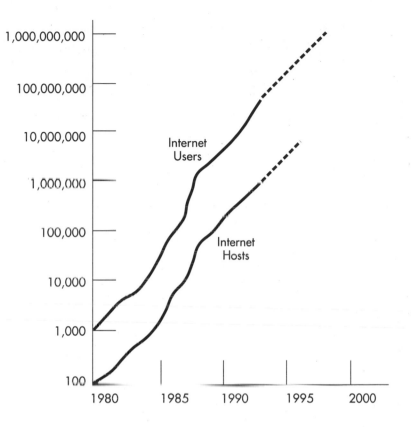

Figure 9. Growth of Internet. (This is a logarithmic plot—equal increments on the vertical axis representing increases by a factor of ten—and, in a logarithmic plot, a straight line, which is roughly what is found here, represents an exponential growth.)

Internet account. Well before then the growth curve will begin turning into an S-curve. The further growth of the net will not then be in the number of connections, but in the versatility and richness of the connections.

As this global network continues to grow and evolve, it will undoubtedly face many crises and will change in many ways. But as we saw in Chapter 5, a system in crisis is not necessarily a dying system. Crises can be important evolutionary drivers pushing the system into new levels of organization, and triggering the emergence of new forms and processes. Already the Internet has proved capable of evolving into a much more complex and diverse structure than that contemplated by its original creators, and, since nobody can turn it off, it will continue to evolve. New technologies, new communication protocols, new software, and other developments will make the net of ten years from now as hard to imagine today as laptop computers talking to each other across the globe were twenty years ago.

MERGING TECHNOLOGIES

At the heart of this proliferation of networks and services is the integration of computer technology and telecommunications. The telephone's global network of cables, fibers and radio links has laid the infrastructure for a new revolution. A telephone socket anywhere in the world—Sweden, Mexico, China, the South Pole—is no longer just a point to attach a device for "hearing at a distance". It is now a node of the network, and can just as easily sport a telex, a fax machine, a pager, a terminal, a computer, a network of computers, or a combination of any of these. Add to this the ability to send video images as easily as text, and you have the seeds for the biggest media revolution ever—the synthesis of television, computer, and telephone.

In the years to come it is not only MIPS that will be important but bandwidth—how fast data can be transmitted through the network. One optic fiber has the potential for 25 gigahertz—which is about the volume of information that flows over the telephone lines in the U.S.A. during the peak moment on Mother's Day, or about 1,000 times more information than all the radio frequencies combined. All that on one thread of glass the width of a human hair.

Just as the price of MIPS has fallen dramatically over the last few decades, so too will the price of bandwidth. George Gilder, author of *Life after Television* and *Telecosm*, has pointed out that every major revolution has seen the cost of some commodity fall markedly and eventually become virtually free. With the Industrial Revolution, physical force became virtually free compared with its cost when derived from animal or human muscle. Suddenly a factory could work 24 hours a day churning out products in a way that was incomprehensible before. Physical force became so cheap that rather than having to economize on its use, we could afford to "waste" it in moving walkways, electric toothbrushes, and leaf blowers. Over the last 30 years we have seen the price of a transistor drop from one dollar to one four-thousandth of a cent. We no longer have to economize on the use of transistors, but can "waste" them to correct our spelling, play solitaire, or create fancy backgrounds on our computer screens. As the telecommunications revolution begins to bite, we will see a similar drop in the cost of bandwidth. When that is virtually free, we will be able to afford to "waste" that, too. We will be able to broadcast information through the net much as we now broadcast radio and television through the air.

Developments such as these seem to be taking us ever

more rapidly towards what William Gibson, in his award-winning novel, *Neuromancer,* called *cyberspace*:

> A graphic representation of data abstracted from the banks of every computer in the human system. Unthinkable complexity. Lines of light ranged in the non-space of the mind, clusters and constellations of data.

In Gibson's world, people enter cyberspace by feeding computer-generated virtual reality displays of information directly into their brains. Science fiction? Yes. But so was a trip to the moon fifty years ago.

THE EMERGING GLOBAL BRAIN

The interlinking of humanity that began with the emergence of language has now progressed to the point where information can be transmitted to anyone, anywhere, at the speed of light. Billions of messages continually shuttle back and forth, in an ever-growing web of communication, linking the billions of minds of humanity together into a single system. Is this Gaia growing herself a nervous system?

The parallels are certainly worthy of consideration. We have already noted that there are, very approximately, the same number of nerve cells in a human brain as there are human minds on the planet. And there are also some interesting similarities between the way the human brain grows and the way in which humanity is evolving.

The embryonic human brain passes through two major phases of development. The first is a massive explosion in the number of nerve cells. Starting eight weeks after conception, the number of neurons explodes, increasing by many millions each hour. After five weeks, however, the process slows down, almost as rapidly as it started. The first stage of brain development, the proliferation of cells, is now complete. At this stage the fetus has most of the nerve cells it will have for the rest of its life.

The brain then proceeds to the second phase of its development, as billions of isolated nerve cells begin making connections with each other, sometimes growing out fibers to connect with cells on the other side of the brain. By the time of birth, a typical nerve cell may communicate directly with several thousand other cells. The growth of the brain after birth consists of the further proliferation of connections. By the time of adulthood many nerve cells are making direct connections with as many as a quarter of a million other cells.

Similar trends can be observed in human society. For the last few centuries the number of "cells" in the embryonic global brain has been proliferating. But today population growth is slowing, and at the same time we are moving into the next phase—the linking of the billions of human minds into a single integrated network. The more complex our global telecommunication capabilities become, the more human society is beginning to look like a planetary nervous system. The global brain is beginning to function.

This awakening is not only apparent to us; it can even be detected millions of miles out in space. Before 1900, any being curious enough to take a "planetary EEG" (i.e., to measure the electromagnetic activity of the planet) would have observed only random, naturally occurring activity, such as that produced by lightning. Today, however, the space around the planet is teeming with millions of different signals, some of them broadcasts to large numbers of people, some of them personal communications, and some of them the chatter of computers exchanging information. As the usable radio bands fill up, we find new ways of cramming information into them, and new spectra of energy, such as light, are being utilized, with the potential of further expanding our communication capacities.

With near-instant linkage of humanity through this communications technology, and the rapid and wholesale dissemination of information, Marshall McLuhan's vision of the world as a global village is fast becoming a reality. From an isolated cottage in a forest in England, I can dial a number in Fiji, and it takes the same amount of time for my voice to reach down the telephone line to Fiji as it does for my brain to tell my finger to touch the dial. As far as time to communicate is concerned, the planet has shrunk so much that the other cells of the global brain are no further away from our brains than are the extremities of our own bodies.

At the same time as the speed of global interaction is increasing, so is the complexity. In 1994 the worldwide telecommunications network had a billion telephones. Yet this network, intricate as it might seem, represents only a minute fraction of the communication terminals in the brain, the trillions of synapses through which nerve cells interact. According to John McNulty, a British computer consultant, the global telecommunications network of 1975 was no more complex than a region of the brain the size of a pea. But overall data-processing capacity is doubling every two and a half years, and if this rate of increase is sustained, the global telecommunications network could equal the brain in complexity by the year 2000. If this seems to be an incredibly rapid development, it is probably because few of us can fully grasp just how fast things are evolving.

The changes that this will bring will be so great that their full impact may well be beyond our imagination. No longer will we perceive ourselves as isolated individuals; we will know ourselves to be a part of a rapidly integrating global network, the nerve cells of an awakened global brain.

CHAPTER 9

AN EMERGING
SOCIAL SUPERORGANISM

We no more know our own destiny than a tea leaf
knows the destiny of the East India Company.
The Hitchhiker's Guide to the Galaxy,
Douglas Adams

The growing complexity that we have just traced within
society reveals three important areas of growth in terms
of evolution: a diversity of human beings; an elaborate or-
ganizational structure, parallel to that observed in all other
living systems; and a communication and information-processing capability approaching that of the human brain.
Society would appear to be completing the prerequisites
for the emergence of a new evolutionary level.

What might this new level look like?

Just as matter became organized into living cells and living cells collected into multicellular organisms, so might we expect that at some stage human beings will become integrated into some form of global social superorganism. (I use the word *superorganism* rather than *organism* since the term organism is usually applied to biological organisms. Here we will be considering not multicellular organisms, but multi-organism organisms.)

A social superorganism, in the sense used here, is more than just a living system. In Chapter 3 we observed that human society seems to display each of the nineteen characteristics of a living system. The same applies to many other social groups—a ship's crew, a multinational company, and the Red Cross. But such groupings are not social superorganisms in the sense of being independent wholes. They are more like constituent organs such as the thyroid gland, the nose, or the liver—living systems that can only exist as part of a larger organism within which they play specific roles. A true social superorganism, like a biological organism, is an independent whole, complete in itself.

Such phenomena are not new to nature. In the animal world there are several examples of organisms that come together to form integrated social units. Thousands of bees may live and work together in a single hive, regulating the temperature and humidity of their collective "body", the hive as a whole surviving the continual birth and death of its members. Army ants form colonies containing up to 20 million individuals. Advancing like a single organism through the forest, a colony will cross streams by forming a living bridge of ants clinging tenaciously to each other.

Termites construct complex cities housing up to several million individuals, complete with ventilation shafts and complex food-processing systems.

Similar tendencies can be found in higher animals. Many fish swim in schools, the whole acting as a single unit without any single leader. Individual fish may take on specific functions, such as that of an "eye", reducing the need for the others to be continually on the lookout. When danger is spotted, a whole school can react in less than a fifth of a second. Flocks of birds can likewise behave like a superorganism. One of the largest ever recorded was a flock of 150 million shearwaters, over ten miles across, observed between Australia and Tasmania. Slow-motion films of bird flocks have revealed 50,000 individuals turning in synchrony in less than a seventieth of a second. There is no indication of their following the leader; the flock is integrated into a functional whole.

But such examples, fascinating as they might be, only afford us a glimpse of the integrated social superorganism that humanity has the potential to become. First, the superorganism will not contain a few million individuals, as occurs with bees, ants, or birds, rather, it will be comprised of the whole human race, billions of individuals distributed over the face of the planet.

Second, in all instances of animal superorganisms there is very little individual diversity. Bee and ant colonies usually contain only two or three different types (e.g., worker bee, drone, queen bee), while in fish and bird groups all the individuals are identical, only temporarily taking on specific functions. Human society, however, is extremely diverse and specialized, made up of thousands of different

types, each able to make his or her own particular contribution to the whole.

Third, a human social superorganism would not en-
tail our all becoming nondescript cells who have given up
their individuality for some higher good. We already are
cells in the various organs that compose society, yet we
still retain considerable individuality. The shift to a social superorganism would mean that society has become
a more integrated living system. As we shall see in later
chapters, this is likely to lead to greater freedom and self-
expression on the part of the individual, and to an even
greater diversity.

Finally, when insects and animals come together, they
congregate as a single unit. But it is extremely unlikely
that the human social superorganism will form itself on
the physical level. From what we have seen of evolutionary trends, we should not anticipate that human beings will
come together as a large conglomerate mass in some
supermegalopolis.

Just as earlier, after life had emerged from matter, evolution moved up from the physical level to the biological
level, so it has now moved up to a new level: consciousness. We could therefore hypothesize that the integration
of society into a superorganism would occur through the
evolution of consciousness rather than through physical or
biological evolution. This implies a coming together of
minds, which is why communication is such an important
aspect of evolution today; it is a mind-linking process.
Humanity is growing together mentally—however distant
we might be physically.

A New Level of Evolution

One philosopher who spent much of his life contemplating the integration of humanity into a single being was the French priest Pierre Teilhard de Chardin. Teilhard displayed that rare synthesis of science and religion: he was both a Jesuit priest and a geologist/paleontologist. In the 1930s he worked in China, where he was closely involved with the discovery of Peking Man. As a result of his study of the evolutionary process, he developed a general theory of evolution that applied not only to the human species but also to the human mind and the relationship of religious experience to the facts of natural science.

One of his principal conclusions was that humanity was headed toward the unification of the entire species into a single interthinking group. He coined the word *noosphere* (from the Greek *noos*, mind) to refer to the cumulative effect of human minds over the entire planet. Just as the biosphere is the system comprised of all living things, so the noosphere is comprised of all conscious minds.

Evolution, having passed through geogenesis (the genesis of the Earth) and biogenesis (the genesis of life), is now at the stage of *noogenesis* (the genesis of the mind). He saw this stage as the "planetization of Mankind . . . [into] a single major organic unity." The fulfillment of this process of noogenesis Teilhard referred to as the *Omega Point*, the culmination of the evolutionary process, the end point toward which we are all converging.

Another philosopher with a similar vision was the Indian mystic Sri Aurobindo, a contemporary of Teilhard's. In him we also find an interesting combination of talents.

He was educated in classics at King's College, Cambridge, and was, on his return to India, an active political revolutionary. As a result he spent several years in Indian jails, and it was during these periods that he had some of his most significant insights into the evolution of humanity.

Sri Aurobindo saw evolution as Divine Reality expressing itself in ever higher forms of existence. Having passed from energy through matter and life to consciousness, evolution was now passing through the transformation from consciousness to what he called "Supermind", something so far above consciousness as to be beyond our present dreams of perfection, the ultimate evolution of Spirit. This new level he saw as coming through the increasing spiritual development of individual consciousness toward a final, complete, all-embracing consciousness, which would occur on both the individual and collective levels.

Since we do not yet have an adequate term in our vocabulary for this new evolutionary phenomenon, I refer to it as the *Gaiafield* (much as self-reflective consciousness might be termed the "human field"). The Gaiafield will not be a property of individual beings any more than consciousness is a property of individual cells. The Gaiafield will occur at the planetary level, emerging from the combined interactions of all the minds within the social superorganism.

Exactly what this new level might be is very difficult to say, because the minute we begin to contemplate a new level of evolution, we inevitably do so in terms of human experience. Since, as we have already seen, each new order of existence is not fully describable in terms of the previous orders, it is likely that the Gaiafield would also possess

entirely new characteristics, unimaginable to our consciousness.

A single cell in the human body knows nothing of the
consciousness that emerges from the living system as a
whole. Although it might have a very rudimentary form of
awareness, it has no conception (if we may excuse the word)
of a person's thoughts, feelings, imagination, or inspiration.
It cannot judge what state of consciousness a person might
be in, or even whether the person is conscious or not. And
it would almost certainly find it impossible to conceive of
what was meant by self-reflective consciousness. So, it is
not altogether surprising if we find it equally difficult to
conceive of evolutionary stages as far beyond us as we are
beyond single cells. Being individuals, the collective phenomena will remain to us unknowable. We only know the
"cell" that we are.

The idea of a collective phenomenon generated from
the activity of our individual consciousness may sound a
little strange. How can many separate consciousnesses give
rise to a single planetary phenomenon? Indeed, the question is similar to the one that scientists and philosophers
continually face with respect to human consciousness: how
do the electrical and chemical activities of many separate
nerve cells give rise to a single integrated consciousness?
All that can be said with any degree of certainty is that the
consciousness of each individual human being is somehow
related to the highly complex and integrated interaction of
billions of living cells in the brain.

Without going into the neurological arguments here, it
seems probable that a particular conscious experience corresponds not to the activity of small groups of cells, but to

overall patterns of activity, to the coherence of the numerous information exchanges continually taking place in the brain. In a similar manner this planetary field would emerge from the integrated interaction of the billions of conscious beings composing humanity. As the communication links within humanity increase, we will eventually reach a time when the billions of information exchanges shuttling through the networks at any one time would create patterns of coherence in the global brain similar to those found in the human brain. Gaia would then awaken and become her equivalent of conscious.

How far away are we from the point in time when this might happen? Teilhard, although he spoke of evolution moving rapidly toward the Omega Point, was thinking in cosmic time scales rather than human ones, and by "rapidly" he seems to have meant thousands or perhaps millions of years. Although towards the end of his life, when he saw the impact of the telephone on social development, Teilhard declared that this would bring the Omega Point much closer. Had he lived long enough to see the impact of the computer, he would probably have declared the Omega Point to have been brought even closer. Sri Aurobindo always believed that it could happen much more quickly, perhaps within the next hundred years.

Yet this new level may well come even faster than either Sri Aurobindo or Teilhard envisioned. It could possibly happen within a few decades.

We have been accustomed to social changes occurring over centuries, or even millennia, and it may be difficult to conceive of something so significant emerging in so short a period. But, as we saw in Chapter 6, the rate of change is rapidly increasing. In this century there has been a massive acceleration in nearly all areas of human endeavor, which could possibly herald some form of major transition in the very near future. Furthermore, the major evolutionary indicators—diversity, organization, and connectivity—are rapidly producing the critical degree of complexity that seems to be needed for a new level to emerge. We shall find, in Part Three, that there are several other reasons for supposing that we might possibly see this shift happening in our own lifetimes.

Such a transition is going to require some very rapid changes on the part of humanity. On the one hand, an individual need only pick up a newspaper to see just how far humanity is from being a cohesive, integrated whole. On the other hand, society is much more than a collection of disassociated individuals going their separate ways. Evolutionarily speaking, we may be in a sort of twilight zone, neither one thing nor the other. As it turns out, this is also a characteristic aspect of evolutionary transitions.

EVOLUTION'S TWILIGHT ZONES

The boundaries between the major evolutionary levels (i.e., energy, matter, life, and consciousness) are not necessarily clear-cut. In between any two appear to be twilight zones where the new order is becoming manifest but has not yet fully emerged.

Looking first at the junction between energy and matter, we find the so-called elementary particles, such as electrons and protons. But are they really matter? In some situations they behave like particles, yet in other situations they behave like waves (behavior more characteristic of energy), a paradox that many physicists have tried to resolve. But when we consider evolution as an emergent process, an elementary particle seems to stand on the borderline between energy and matter; it is matter emerging from energy, a halfway stage.

Between the next two levels, between matter and life, are the viruses and macromolecules such as DNA. Here the question is: Are they alive? In some respects they are, since they can, under suitable circumstances, reproduce themselves. But they can also form regular crystals, behaving like many of the simpler molecules. They seem to be in the twilight zone where matter has not yet become sufficiently organized to lead to the emergence of true life.

A similar twilight zone appears to exist between life and self-reflective consciousness. In this case it is occupied by primates such as chimpanzees. Like other animals, they are conscious, in the sense of being aware of their surroundings. But are they conscious of themselves and conscious that they are conscious? The answer is not clear-cut. Chimpanzees and a few other primates, such as orangutans, are different from other animals in that they display a degree of self-recognition. When they see an image of themselves in a mirror they realize that they are seeing themselves rather than another animal of the same species. Furthermore, in a number of studies chimps have been taught various sign languages. Some of those chimps appear to display a rudimentary self-consciousness; they are able to refer to themselves by name, and express how they are feeling. They would appear, therefore, to be somewhere in the twilight zone that precedes the emergence of true self-reflective consciousness.

At the present time, evolution seems to have reached yet another twilight zone, the one between consciousness and the Gaiafield. Humanity currently displays characteristics of both levels: we are independent, conscious units, who at times come together to function as an integrated whole for a common purpose. In this respect, society is reminiscent of a curious creature, the cellular slime mold *Dictyostelium discoideum*, an "organism" which is somewhere between a collection of single-celled amoeba and a true multicellular organism.

Most of the time the separate amoeba constituting a slime mold roam around old bits of wood and dead leaves, looking for bacteria on which to feed and multiplying as they go. Should the food supply become scarce, the separate amoeba start clustering into small groups of a few dozen individuals. These groupings then conglomerate into a single blob, called a grex, often containing thousands of amoeba. Having come together, some of the cells begin climbing on top of the others until they form a hemispherical dome, which develops into a cone with a "nipple" on top. The whole then falls over onto its side and becomes a small "slug" able to move across the forest floor in the direction of light, the nipple raised and leading the way.

If food is found, the grex may dissolve again into thousands of individual amoeba going off on their own. If not, it may turn up on its end, thousands of amoeba climbing on top of each other to become a thin vertical stalk as much as an inch in height. At the top of this thin stalk other amoeba will form into a small sphere and become spores to be cast off and carried away in the air. If an amoeba lands where there is an abundant supply of food, it begins reproducing and spreading as before—until, that is, the food supply begins to become exhausted, whereupon the whole process begins over again.

Parallel behaviors are found in human societies, both primitive and advanced. The Kachin people of northern Burma, for example, who have been studied extensively by the British anthropologist, Edmund Leach, spend most of their time in separate tribal communities. When food is scarce, however, they come together as a unit under one king and stay as a single community until times improve. Similarly, in the more developed Western nations, when there are no major catastrophes, each person mainly pursues his own interests. But should there be a disaster, such as a widespread famine, flood, or war, people may begin acting more in the group interest, and society takes on more of the characteristics of an integrated organism.

EMERGENCE THROUGH EMERGENCY

To say that humanity is in the twilight zone is not to imply that the emergence of the next level is inevitable. Transition periods are fraught with danger, and this is clearly the case with society today. We are deeply entangled in the most complex web of social, political, economic, ecological, and moral crises in human history. Will these crises prevent the emergence of a new level of evolution? Perhaps. Certainly we have any number of doomsday projections that explore the possibilities of apocalypse in detail. But our earlier review of evolution revealed quite another possible scenario: that crisis may be an evolutionary catalyst in the push toward a higher level.

Initially, any crisis seems painful and dangerous, and one's immediate reaction may be to try to stop it, holding on as firmly as possible to the old order. But if there is a possibility of a new order emerging from this crisis, hanging on to the current state may be counterproductive, perhaps even deepening the problem. To use an analogy of futurist Barbara Marx Hubbard, imagine what a committee of bacteria would have said about the environmental impact of a small group of bacteria's plans to use photosynthesis, 3,500 million years ago: "The oxygen produced by this process is dangerous stuff. It is poisonous to all known forms of life, and it is also highly inflammable, likely to burn us all to ashes. It is almost certain to lead to the destruction of life." Without doubt, photosynthesis would have been banned as "selfish, unnatural, and irresponsible." Luckily for us, no such committee existed, and photosynthesis went on ahead. It did indeed bring about a major crisis, but on the other side of it came plants, animals, and you and me.

The set of global problems that humanity is facing presently may turn out to be as important to our continued evolution as "the oxygen crisis" was. Never in the history of the human race have the dangers been so extreme; yet in their role as evolutionary catalysts, they may be just what is needed to push us to a higher level.

The idea that crises have both negative and positive aspects is captured in a word the Chinese have found for crises, wei-chi. The first part of the word means "beware, danger".

The second part, however, has a very different implication; it means "opportunity for change".

The concept of wei-chi allows us to appreciate the importance of both aspects of crisis. In recent years, our attention has generally been focused on the *wei*, on the many possibilities for global catastrophe and how to avoid them. This will continue to be necessary as we strive to deal with the very real problems that face us. At the same time, these crises may lead us to question some of our basic attitudes and values: Why are we here? What do we *really* want? Isn't there more to life? This questioning opens us up to the other aspect of crisis, *chi:* the opportunity to change direction, to benefit from the prodigious and breathtaking possibilities that could be before us.

PART THREE

INNER
EVOLUTION

CHAPTER 10

SYNERGY

> People travel to wonder at the height of mountains, at the huge waves of the sea, at the long courses of rivers, at the vast compass of the ocean, at the circular motion of the stars; and they pass by themselves without wondering.
> *St. Augustine, A.D. 399*

What we have traced so far is society's increasing complexity and the many indicators that we could now be living through the most dramatic and crucial period of human history: the progressive integration of human minds into a single living system—a global brain.

Yet we do not have to look far to see that humanity today is also on the brink of disaster. Paradoxically, the very same technological, scientific, and social advances that have pushed us so far forward may also contain the seeds of our demise. We appear to be wavering precariously between two mutually exclusive directions: breaking through to become a global social superorganism or breaking down into chaos and possible extinction.

Clearly, given the choice, most people would not opt consciously for catastrophe. Nevertheless, as a group we seem to be drifting in that direction. Unable to fathom the complexity of the society we have become, we seem powerless to steer it in the direction we would want it to go. Why is this? Why are we not more like the organism we have the potential to be?

The answer lies in what characterizes a successfully functioning organism. When we look at organisms that work—and just about every organism apart from human society does work—we find that there is one particular quality that they all share: the many components naturally and spontaneously function together, in harmony with the whole. This characteristic can be seen operating in organisms as different as a slime mold, an oak tree, or the human body. This harmonious interaction can be described by the word *synergy,* derived from the Greek *syn-ergos,* meaning "to work together".

Synergy does not imply any coercion or restraint, nor is it brought about by deliberate effort. Each individual element of the system works toward its own goals, and the goals themselves may be quite varied. Yet the elements function in ways that are *spontaneously* mutually supportive. Consequently, there is little, if any, intrinsic conflict.

The word synergy has sometimes been used in the sense of the whole being greater than the sum of its parts. But this is not the word's root meaning; this interpretation is a consequence of synergy in its original sense. Because the elements in a synergistic system support each other, they also support the functioning of the system as a whole, and the performance of the whole is improved.

An excellent example of a system with high synergy is your own body. You are an assortment of several trillion individual cells, each acting for its own interest, yet each simultaneously supporting the good of the whole. A skin cell in your finger is doing its job as a skin cell, taking in various nourishments, getting rid of its waste products, and living and dying as a skin cell. It is not directly concerned with what is happening to a skin cell in your toe or to what is happening to your bone cells, brain cells, or muscle cells. It is simply looking after its own interests. Yet, its own interests are also the general interests of other cells in the body, and the activity of the organism as a whole. If it were not for this high degree of synergy, each of us would be just a mass of jelly, each cell acting only for itself and not contributing to the rest of the body.

Synergy in an organism is the essence of life, and it is intimately related to health. When for some reason synergy drops and the organism as a whole does not receive the full support of its many parts, it becomes ill. When synergy is lost altogether, the organism dies. The individual cell may live on, but the whole, the *living* organism, no longer exists.

Likewise in social groups, synergy represents the extent to which the activities of the individual support the group as a whole. Anthropologists studying primitive tribal systems have found that groups high in synergy tend to be low in conflict and aggression, both between individuals and between individuals and the group. This does not mean that such societies are full of "do-gooders" desperately trying to help each other; rather, they are societies in which the social and psychological structures are such that the activity of the individual is naturally in tune with the needs of others and the needs of the group.

Viewed as a system, human society today would appear to be in a state of comparatively low synergy. As we shall see shortly, many of the crises now facing us may be symptomatic of this deeper, underlying problem. Yet as much as we might want increased synergy in society, it will not come about simply through desire, intellectual decision, argument, or coercion. The amount of synergy in a society is a *reflection* of the way in which we perceive ourselves in relation to the world around us. In order to increase synergy, then, we will need to change some fundamental assumptions that lie at the core of our thinking and behavior. This will mean evolving inwardly as much as we have done outwardly.

The spearhead of evolution is now self-reflective consciousness. If evolution is indeed to push on to yet higher levels of integration, the most crucial changes will take place in the realm of human consciousness. In effect the evolutionary process has now become internalized within each of us. To see what this means, and how we may evolve inwardly, let us start by looking at how our internal model of ourselves governs our perception, thinking, and action.

CHAPTER 11

THE SKIN-ENCAPSULATED EGO

Two birds,
inseparable companions,
perch on the same tree.
One eats the fruit,
the other looks on.

The first bird is our individual self,
feeding on the pleasures and pains
of this world.
The other is the universal Self,
silently witnessing all.
　　　Mundaka Upanishad, 5th Century B.C.

For thousands of years people believed that the sun went around the Earth. So widespread and firm was this belief that it was taken to be reality. In the sixteenth century, however, Copernicus put forward the radically different idea that the Earth went around the sun. His theory was not readily accepted. It took a century of haggling before the old reality was scrapped and a new reality adopted.

This complete reversal in world view did not come about through the discovery of any fundamentally new data, but through the interpretation of existing data in a new way. Clearly, the motion of the planets had not changed; what changed was the conceptual perspective through which their motion was viewed.

Scientists speak of this process as the creation of a new paradigm, a term coined by the philosopher and science historian Thomas Kuhn in his book *The Structure of Scientific Revolutions.* The word *paradigm,* derived from the Greek *paradigma* ("pattern"), was used by Kuhn to refer to the dominant theoretical framework, or set of assumptions, that underlies any particular science. A paradigm is like a "super theory" providing the basic model of reality within a particular science. It governs the way a scientist thinks and theorizes and the way in which experimental observations are interpreted.

Once accepted, paradigms are seldom questioned; they usually become self-perpetuating scientific dogma. As a result, scientists tend to accept phenomena that fit in with the model and reject those that do not. However, there occasionally comes a time when the phenomena that do not fit become so evident that they can no longer be ignored. This usually results in what Kuhn referred to as a "paradigm shift", a change in a world view—something that we will be looking at in more detail later.

Although Kuhn originally put forward the idea of paradigms in relation to scientific thought, his ideas have been applied to many other areas: education, economics, sociology, politics, health care, and our world view in general. The principles can also be applied to the way in which we perceive reality and relate to ourselves.

Underlying our thoughts, perceptions, and experiences are implicit assumptions about the way the world is. In seeing, for example, the eyes supply the brain with sensory data about the world "out there". But before this data can give rise to a meaningful experience, it first has to be interpreted and organized by the brain, and this requires a model of the world (i.e., an idea of how things are). On its own, without these perceptual frameworks, the raw visual data remain meaningless, as shown by the illustration on the following page.

If you have not seen Figure 10 before, it will probably appear as a random assortment of black and white patches.

It is, in fact, a picture of a face, a rather medieval-looking, bearded man. Without a visual model of what the face looks like, however, few people are able to see it at first glance.

Look at the illustration for a minute or so and if you still cannot see the face (as many people cannot), then take a look at the figure on page 189. You should now have a satisfactory visual model with which to interpret the incoming sensory data and so "see" the face in Figure 10. Moreover, you will probably always see it so long as you remember what it should look like, that is, so long as you retain the model.

Psychologists refer to the mental models that underlie the construction of perception as "sets". They not only condition most of our experience, they also determine what

Figure 10. A random array of black and white patches? An aerial photograph of Baffin Island? A picture of a face? Without a mental model of what it actually is, it may be difficult to tell.

is reality for each of us. We are predisposed by our sets to see certain features in our environment more than others. If, for example, you have just bought a new car, you will probably start seeing a lot more of those cars on the streets, particularly ones of the same color. You might think that the market has suddenly been flooded with them. But the number of such cars has not changed; what has happened is that your mind has become "set" for them and notices them much more readily.

Mental sets can influence our behavior and performance. An athlete who is convinced she can establish a new world record, for instance, is more likely to achieve this goal than an athlete of equal capability who has the set that the record is virtually unbeatable.

They can also affect our emotional reality. A depressed person who feels that no one respects or loves him and that the whole world is out to get him has a negative mental set. Experiences and conversations are interpreted in a pessimistic light; positive, supportive comments are dismissed or undervalued; and the personal reality of gloom becomes self-reinforcing.

Similarly, the way in which we evaluate the world is affected by set. If our general set is of impending economic collapse, of international tension and aggression leading sooner or later to World War III, of potential disasters and famines, then we will be more likely to notice those elements when reported by the media, with the effect that the negative set will be reinforced. Moreover, we are also likely to act in ways that support that set. Like the athlete who does not really believe he can set a new record, we will help bring about a self-fulfilling prophecy.

In short, mental sets, whether we are aware of their presence or not, are extremely powerful. They determine how sensory data are to be interpreted, which experiences to accept as real and which to reject as illusion, and what reality is like. Like paradigms, they are usually taken for granted and seldom, if ever, questioned.

SELF-MODELS

Underlying how we think the world works (paradigms) and how we construct our experience (sets) is an even more basic model: the way in which we see ourselves and the relationship between this self and everything else. This fundamental model conditions *all* thought, perception, and action. It is the set, or paradigm, for all mental activity. Furthermore, since a self-model is often implicit in many educational, social, economic, and political paradigms, it can even condition the development of paradigms themselves. If a physicist, for instance, experiences his consciousness and the physical world to be completely separate entities, he is likely to evolve different paradigms than if he experienced the two as part of a greater whole. In this respect our self-model is more than a set or paradigm. It could be termed a *meta* set or *meta* paradigm (from the Greek *meta,* beyond), that which lies beyond all other sets and paradigms. Whereas a paradigm is a framework for thinking, the metaparadigm of our self-model is a framework for being.

The most common self-model, the metaparadigm by which most of us operate, is that of a unique individual self quite separate from the rest of the world and quite distinct from other selves. Functioning within this model, we go about our daily lives with the assumption that "I" am "in here", while the rest of the world is "out there." The philosopher and theologian Alan Watts dubbed this the "skin-encapsulated ego": What is inside the skin is "I", what is outside is "not I." All our perceptions and experiences, according to Watts, are interpreted on this basis, and we model reality accordingly. This view of the self is so pervasive that few people ever realize it is just a model, or notice its effects upon their experience and thinking.

But this model of self is not the only one. A radically different, yet complementary, model is also possible, that of a universal self not bounded by the skin or distinguishable from other selves, a self whose essential quality is oneness with the rest of creation, rather than separation from it.

Although experiences of this universal self are not as rare as one might suppose, it is extremely rare indeed to have this universal self be the dominant self-model through which a person perceives the world. The skin-encapsulated model is by far the prevalent model. Yet it may very well be that it is this model that lies at the root of much of humanity's problems today. To understand just how deeply rooted it is, let us look at how this model develops.

THE DEVELOPMENT OF DUALITY

The newborn baby is aware of the environment but does not appear to differentiate himself from it. He is not aware of himself as a separate entity. As awareness of physical separateness from the mother begins to grow, so does the awareness of separateness from the rest of the environment. According to most psychologists, a true sense of individuality does not come about until simple language has begun to develop— some, such as Jean Piaget, would claim that full identity of the self is not attained until the age of seven or eight. This feeling of individuality is reinforced by most languages: the subject-object relationship inherent in their noun-verb structure implies that the actor and action are quite separate and distinct. This becomes manifest in the growing child's subtle but important shift from: "John wants the ball," to "I want the ball." The child begins to be conscious of an internal self.

In addition to learning a dualistic language, the growing child learns from his parents how to think and behave. If the parents project the assumption that "I" am "in here", completely separate from the environment "out there", then the child learns to adopt the same model and begins to develop his own thinking along the same lines. So the skin-encapsulated ego develops.

The sense of discreteness and uniqueness given by this model does have considerable value. Biologically speaking, we are very much self-maintaining, self-regulating, self-directing organisms, and the notion of a separate individual self is a symbol of this autonomy. The feeling of uniqueness that comes with a sense of a discrete self allows us to distinguish our own selves from others. In addition, striving to maintain a unique, individual self ensures a much higher chance of survival for the physiological organism.

At the psychological level, this sense of individuality

provides an inner unity to all thought, feeling, perception, and action. It is I "in here" who is experiencing and doing. This gives us our sense of "I-ness".

When the skin-encapsulated self is taken as the *only* sense of self, however, we end up seeing the world solely in terms of "I" and "not I". This leads us to feel there is an absolute distinction between ourselves and others. We characterize ourselves through the ways in which we appear to each other and draw our separate identities from those features—height, weight, age, sex, nationality, skin color, clothes, house, car, social status, job, friends, character, personality, thoughts, and ideologies—which distinguish us from others. Thus a sense of who we are appears to be derived from our perceptions, experiences, and interactions with the external world, from the ways in which we are different from others.

Yet the self is not really any of these things. A person can be of a different height, weight, age, etc., but this does not make his sense of "I-ness" different. It seems that we derive a sense of self from what we are not.

Deriving our identity in this way is, to borrow an analogy from the American philosopher Daniel Cowan, like describing a hole in a piece of wood in terms of the color, shape, and texture of the wood that surrounds the hole (e.g., "it is a brown, round, smooth hole"). The hole's identity is, so to speak, derived from the wood around it. Most people describe a hole in this way because the qualities of the hole itself are much more abstract; it is easier to describe the qualities of the wood than the transparent air that fills the hole. Similarly, our sense of personal identity is usually derived from what surrounds the self (i.e., from our expe-

rience of the world). What lies within is much more difficult to describe.

When an externally derived sense of identity is our only
sense of identity, it becomes the most precious of possessions. Without it "I" would, quite literally, cease to be.
(This is a major reason why physical death is so greatly
feared: it implies the separation from everything that one
has depended upon for a sense of self.) Yet the derived self
is as transitory and ephemeral as the experiences from which
it is derived. It needs continual maintenance, nurturing,
and protection, and people will often go to great lengths to
ensure it gets this sustenance. Much of human activity is
geared to establishing and defending our identities, and
much of the low synergy we observe in society can be traced
back to this need.

To Be Loved, To Belong, and To Believe

Deriving our sense of identity from our interaction with
others, we need people to recognize and reaffirm our existence and frequently spend considerable effort fulfilling this
need. Life becomes a search for personal reinforcement
(what are often termed positive psychological *strokes*).
There is not necessarily anything wrong in this; it certainly
does make us feel good. But if strokes are the mainstay of
our sense of well-being, the search for them can consume a
vast amount of time and energy. Some psychologists esti-
mate that as much as 80 percent of our interactions with
other people come from the need for reinforcement.

At the same time, our vulnerability to emotional injury

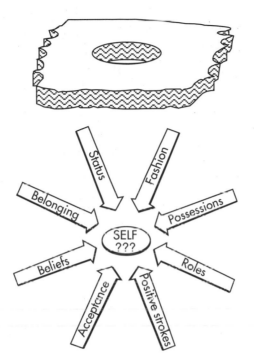

Figure 11. When asked to describe a hole in a piece of wood, people often do so in terms of the qualities of the wood that surrounds it. Similarly the self, when it is not known in its own right, is usually defined in terms of its surroundings.

is very high; the derived self is extremely fragile. Events are seldom seen as neutral, and what is not reinforcing is usually seen as threatening. As a result, time not spent pursuing positive strokes may be spent avoiding negative strokes.

When we do receive negative strokes we feel hurt, and the result is often unhappiness and depression. A study of melancholy by Gerald Klerman showed that "the main forces that initiate depressive responses are threats to the psychological integrity of the individual, to the sense of self," and concluded that melancholy and depression are the most common psychological complaints of our times.

Another way in which the derived self handles negative strokes, particularly criticism, is to call up its psychological defense mechanisms, such as rationalization, blocking, and retaliation—methods the injured identity uses to make itself strong again. But since this reinforcement/protection process never fully satisfies the self's hunger for reaffirmation, most people unconsciously use many other tactics to bolster their sense of identity. One of these is gathering possessions.

We acquire possessions to show who we are, to give ourselves some status. Personal identity often comes to be measured in terms of material possessions, whether they be houses, cars, TV sets, CDs, laptop computers, paintings, libraries, furniture, or whatever. When the status connected to a particular possession drops off, it may be discarded or exchanged for something with a little more prestige. The need to trade in last year's car for next year's model, for example, is usually born of the need to sustain a sense of who we are rather than provide a more satisfactory means of transportation. In line with this, many advertisements prey upon the need to reaffirm a sense of self. (Buy a certain model of car and you can be like the good-looking, supercool, immaculately dressed owner, admired by everyone. Of course, you may not completely fit the bill, but the intention is for you to feel you are more that sort of person, as you identify with that image.)

The derived self, constantly striving to reaffirm its existence, often finds added security by identifying with something larger, such as a group or belief system. Belonging to a particular group, whether it be a social group, political group, religious group, or private club provides the derived self with the feeling of "safety in numbers". Similarly, people live in the "right" parts of town, belong to the "right" clubs, know the "right" people, drive the "right" cars, go to the "right" places for their vacation, wear the "right" clothes, listen to the "right" music, and even smoke the "right" cigarettes, not because any of them is necessarily better, but because they support one's identity with a particular group.

Fashion likewise depends on the need to reaffirm our sense of self. About twenty years ago there was a craze for platform shoes, with as much as four inches of block between the foot and the ground. Such shoes caught on, not because everybody was clamoring for such footwear, but because it was presented as fashion, and to be in fashion was to belong to the "right" group. (This fashion in particular had the added bonus of making the wearer several inches higher, boosting the ego even further.) Millions of people succumbed to platform shoes, even though they caused countless twisted ankles and injured backs. The derived self evidently considered these disabilities a fair tradeoff for the reaffirmation of belongingness.

Such behavior may be relatively harmless to society as a whole, but the need to belong to a group can lead to much more serious problems. As soon as another group appears which threatens their sense of belongingness, people can change dramatically. When, for example, a group of a different color moves into a town, otherwise peaceful citizens may suddenly become antagonistic, verbally aggressive, and even physically violent. Adam Curle, professor of peace studies at the University of Bradford, points out that this "belonging-identity is the motive force for xenophobia; for the mindless patriotism of 'my country, right or wrong'; for the pseudomystical yearning after blood and soil; for the arrogant superiority of the local man over the stranger. It is an attribute which we all finally share, and in doing so contribute to the most dangerous dilemma of the human race."

Another strong source of identity is our beliefs, which we will go to great lengths to defend. When they are questioned, the derived self may feel threatened, often triggering strong emotional reactions as we struggle to preserve the status of our own viewpoint, or attack opposing views. Even when we think we are arguing rationally, we may bring to our aid a number of ingenious devices—selective perception, diversion, appealing to authority, misrepresentation, defamation, blinding with facts or jargon—to prove we are right.

But the repercussions to holding on to beliefs as part of one's identity can extend dangerously far. Governments often will stick rigidly to their policies, even though these policies may no longer be viable, rather than admit their political beliefs might be wrong. Some of the most bitter and bloody wars in history have been fought in the defense of belief systems.

CHAPTER 12

LOW-SYNERGY SOCIETY

A great many people will think they are thinking
when they are merely rearranging their prejudices.
William James

The need to sustain and reaffirm a sense of identity
derived from experience whether through the
search for reaffirming strokes, the roles we play, the groups
we join, the beliefs we adopt, or some other process—can
lead us to use the world to feed the self. This results in an
exploitive mode of consciousness. We become exploiters
of our surroundings, of other people, and even of our own
bodies. This mode of consciousness lies at the core of the
low-synergy society.

The essence of synergy is that the goals of the individual
are supportive of the group's goals. But the need to main-

tain a derived sense of identity is often in conflict with the best interests of other people and those of the group as a whole. Like a child, the derived self needs immediate gratification, and this inevitably leads to the sacrifice of long-term goals in the pursuit of short-term benefits: the antithesis of synergistic behavior.

One example of low synergy is people topping up their fuel tanks at the first murmur of a cutback in oil supply. The individual need is to avoid running out of fuel, so everyone takes in a few extra gallons, and the excess load on the supply system results in the filling stations' running dry, creating a very real fuel crisis. The individual's action is clearly not in the group interest.

THE PROBLEM OF THE COMMONS

This conflict between the short-term needs of the individual and the long-term goals of the group as a whole leads to what ecologists refer to as the "problem of the commons". The commons were originally the common pastures used for grazing, but the term is now used to refer to jointly owned resources such as the oceans and the atmosphere. The problem of the commons occurs when people are taking resources out of the pool faster than they are replenishing them—harvesting whales, for example, faster than they can reproduce. It might be in the short-term interest of any individual or group to grasp what he can as fast as he can, but it is clearly not in the long-term interest of everyone else. It will lead to the ultimate collapse of that resource, with nothing more left for anyone, including the original taker.

To try to solve the problem of the commons, psychologists have experimented with various simulation games. Julian Edney, an environmental psychologist who has been working on this at Yale, found that after people experience the simulated downfall of the commons many times, they learn (but only gradually) to curtail individual needs in order to ensure their long-term survival. In the real world, however, we cannot afford to see the food supplies, fossil fuels, and other common resources collapse even once, let alone a hundred times. We cannot afford to learn by experience.

The indications are that, in the not-too-distant future, the more developed nations are going to have to cut back on their consumption of oil and other raw materials. Yet, so long as personal identity is strongly bolstered by consumer goods and material luxuries, people are not going to take kindly to the idea of a less consumptive life-style. Most of us *understand* that we have to reduce our oil consumption; but without strict rationing or exorbitant price increases, few people are voluntarily going to cut their fuel consumption while they still derive a strong sense of identity from driving their own particular car. It would seem that our need for ego-support leads us to resist the changes we most need.

This dilemma is related to what sociologists sometimes call the "free-rider problem". This arises when a person perceives himself as a separate, independent individual, taking the attitude that, "What I do will not have any effect on the collective." A person may, for example, decide to avoid paying part of his taxes. The loss to the government may be less than a millionth of 1 percent, and neither the government nor anyone else in the nation is going to know the difference. The tax avoider not only gains financially but also continues to enjoy the benefit of all the public services financed by the tax money of others.

The lack of any obvious solution to this problem has been used as an argument for coercive legislation, to force people to forsake their individual goals. But this only patches over the real conflict. As long as a person's dominant need is to take care of the self, he will only go along with the collective goals because he fears for his own welfare or because he is concerned about the esteem of his fellows.

In some senses, the free-rider is right: he personally does benefit and no one individual suffers as a result of his actions. Yet if everybody followed this argument it would be disastrous. The distinction between the self and the world can lead to an "I versus you" approach to life, both on a personal and national level. People vie with each other to stay top dog; scientists keep their work secret so they can be the first to publish; high-rise housing goes empty while people go homeless because the situation is in the interest of the owner; Catholics and Protestants blow each other up because they cannot live together; nations fight over resources because they cannot share them; rich countries hoard grain while poorer peoples starve, because it's in their own economic and political interest.

Some people might argue that "the system" is to blame for the problems that arise from competitive, or ego-centered, behavior of individuals or nations. But when today's crises are viewed in the light of the derived self, it seems just as likely that the shortcomings of society reflect the state of consciousness of the people who compose it, and that the self creates the system as much as the system creates the self.

THE INVINCIBLE HAND OF SELF-INTEREST

Two hundred years ago the philosopher and political economist Adam Smith realized that the drive to maintain personal security was the basic force behind capitalism. He argued that the individual, by looking after his own interests, would be "led by an invisible hand. . . without intending it, to advance the interest of the society." His theories depicted a society that would naturally be high in synergy.

Unfortunately, capitalist society has not turned out entirely as Smith theorized. He assumed that individuals would act in their own long-term interests. What he failed to take into account was how our egos often seek short-term or even immediate reinforcement, rather than long-term benefit. Consequently individuals may often act against their own real interests and against those of society as a whole.

In his book *Adam Smith's Mistake*, Kenneth Lux shows how Smith was concerned with the relative merits of self-interest and benevolence, and argued that the invisible hand of self-interest generally did more for the common good (and for the individual good) than altruistic, self-sacrificing benevolence. His mistake, as Lux so clearly points out, was to argue in favor of self-interest alone, disregarding benevolence. If we were all enlightened human beings this might work. But we are not. Not all of us, for example, are honest. If a merchant can cheat a customer (say by using short weights on his scale) *and get away with it*, then it is in his self-interest to do so. Self-interest does not rule out cheating; it only decrees that one should not get caught.

The same goes for theft, fraud, and other deceptive acts. Societies worldwide are littered with people whose self-interest has led them to behave in ways that clearly do not promote the common good.

Corruption not only undermines our society, it also undermines our attempts to care for the environment. What large development project in Africa, Latin America, or Asia in the past three decades has gone ahead without a large kickback to politicians? Developing countries complain about their onerous debt burden. Brazil, for example, has to service the interest on more than $100 billion of loans. But each year $50 billion quietly slips out of the country into various foreign bank accounts—enough to repay most of the country's debt in a couple of years.

Capitalism is not the only economic system that suffers from the weaknesses of the derived sense of self; communism, too, is subject to it. Whereas capitalism surrenders to the needs of the ego, communism (and I am speaking here of the brand of communism that was practiced in the former Soviet Union and most Eastern European countries) made the opposite error. It failed to take the needs of the self into account. This is one reason why it collapsed.

Marxist theory held that each person be supported according to his needs. But the most urgent personal needs, the needs of the identity, were ignored or derided. The communist system could be made to work only through the suppression of the individual self. Collective action and national support had to be maintained through propaganda that, like capitalist advertising, preyed upon the need to reaffirm an identity. Psychological sustenance was still gained through belongingness—in this case belonging to the right type of state. But the needs of the derived sense of self could not be suppressed forever, and when the system collapsed, they reappeared with a vengeance. Extortion, fraud, corruption, and organized crime took to the streets, threatening to suffocate the nascent free-enterprise system in its first breath.

Although their intention is commendable, the communist system is of no higher synergy than the capitalist one. In neither case are the needs of the individual in tune with the needs of society as a whole. In a capitalist state, the needs of the individual dominate and the society as a whole stands to lose (and ultimately the individual as well). In the communist state the needs of society dominate and the individual stands to lose (and ultimately the state as well). Regardless of the system, the personal reality is still one of I am "in here" and the world is "out there". It is still a case of I versus you.

HUMANITY VERSUS NATURE

The dangerous separation of ourselves from others, so symptomatic of the low-synergy society, has led us to an even deeper schism: the "I versus it" approach to the world, characterized in Western culture as "humanity versus nature". This approach has been strongly reinforced by scientific and technological models that see humanity as the supreme life-form, able to exercise control over the world and tame it to its own ends. Yet it is not science and technology themselves that are to blame for our present critical situation, but the way in which they have been used. In most cases they serve individual, corporate, and national egos rather than humanity and the planet. Nations cannot be more synergistic than the individuals who comprise them, and so they, too, fall victim to limited and shortsighted goals.

Sulfur dioxide released into the U.S. skies falls as acid rain in Canada. Toxic substances thrown into our rivers are washed out to sea, and end up in the fish on our table. We steadily tear down giant forests, removing the planet's prime source of oxygen and destroying the natural habitat of millions of different species. Such behavior may satisfy our short-term needs, but it does not take into account what will happen when the trees run out and the fish are all dead, nor the long-term damage we could be doing to the biosphere. Countries continue to plan the building of nuclear reactors, even though no one can guarantee that a major accident will not contaminate the planet. We leave a legacy of potential disaster just because it suits our immediate aims.

When things go wrong and nature fails to follow our plan, we devise a *fix* to patch over the flaws in our approach so that we can continue onward. European agribusiness, knowing better than nature, fixed the inefficiency of the old rotation system by becoming intensive, ripping out hedges, and cramming in crops. They then fixed the ecosystem they had damaged with extra fertilizers. New hybrids were developed to raise crop yields, yet these now rely heavily on oil for the special fertilizers and pesticides on which their survival depends. It now takes about fifty times as much energy (mostly oil) to produce the food we eat as we get from eating it. What will happen when the oil runs out? Probably another technological fix—although we should not count on it.

A NEW WORLD VIEW

For nearly every problem facing humanity, we have the knowledge necessary to change course and avoid catastrophe, or, if we do not have it yet, we know how to proceed in order to gain it. We have, for example, the knowledge and most of the technology whereby we could, over a ten-year period, make the shift from fossil fuels to renewable resources such as hydroelectricity, tidal energy, wind power, geothermal energy, and solar energy, to satisfy the major part of the world's energy requirements. Yet the proportion of the developed nations' energy budget spent on research and development of renewable resources is less than one percent of that spent on furthering our dependence on the rapidly dwindling supplies of oil.

The real problem lies not in the physical constraints imposed by the external world but in the constraints of our own minds. The currently predominant world view seems to be that of man, the dominator and manipulator of nature, inherently aggressive and nationalistic, with the principal goals of productivity, material progress, economic efficiency, and growth. Science is viewed as the ultimate source of knowledge, and technology as the means to achieve everything.

Although widely held within the developed nations, this

world view has only been with us for the last few centuries.
It emerged with the Industrial Revolution as a shift away
from the predominantly ecclesiastical model of the Middle
Ages, which saw religious teachings rather than science as
the source of knowledge and God as the supreme arbitra-
tor. Valuable though it may have been, our current model
no longer seems to be working. And as the old model is
losing its usefulness, it is beginning to threaten our continued existence on this planet. Moreover, the longer we cling
to the old world view, the greater the chances we will end
up where we are currently headed.

If, by altering our world view, we are to avert a collective catastrophe, then some major and fundamental changes
will be necessary: changes in the way we relate to ourselves,
our bodies, and surroundings; changes in our needs;
changes in the demands we make of others and of the planet;
and changes in our awareness and appreciation of the world.
As numerous people have pointed out, a new world view is
needed, one that is holistic, nonexploitive, ecologically sound,
long-term, global, peaceful, humane, and cooperative. This
would mean a shift to a truly global perspective, one in which
the individual, the society, and the planet are all given full
recognition, in other words, a shift from a world view that is
low in synergy to one that is high in synergy.

It has been suggested here that the root cause of much
of the low synergy in contemporary society is our use of
the skin-encapsulated model of the self for the mainstay of
our identity. Until recently, there had been little reason to
question this dualist model; it seemed to work fairly satisfactorily, and most languages and cultural traditions
supported it. But the gravity of the rapidly growing global

crises are helping us to see that it contains some fundamental flaws.

To change the global situation, far more than a series of social, scientific, and technological paradigm shifts would seem to be called for. To shift from a low- to a high-synergy society will require a shift in metaparadigm, a profound shift in our basic self-model. Such a change in consciousness has now become an evolutionary imperative.

This does not imply that we must rid ourselves of the skin-encapsulated model. We are very much unique biological organisms, perceiving and acting upon the environment, with strong motivations to protect and nourish this individuality.

Yet this is only one side of the self. Spiritual teachers, mystics, and visionaries have repeatedly affirmed, whatever their culture or time, that we are more than just biological organisms bounded by skin. We are also unbounded, part of a greater wholeness, united with the rest of the universe. This is the other side of our identity, that aspect of the self that can balance out our sense of individuality and separateness. It is to the nature and the means of unfolding this deeper identity that we shall now turn.

CHAPTER 13

THE QUEST FOR UNITY

Yes, there is That which is the end of understanding
Yes, there is That which you will only understand
At the mind's flowering time
When she shall leaf and bud and burst
Into her fullest inflorescence of fine flowers
But should you try to trammel up the mind,
And bind her, confine her, and *strive* to turn her inwards
You will not understand

For there is a power of the mind's prime
Which, rising like the sun in all his majesty,
Shines forth with rays of thought at one with feeling.
Hold still the vision of thy Soul in purity
Freed from all else
Let but thy little mind be empty of all things else
All things save one—thine aim
To reach the end of understanding
For that subsists beyond the mind.

The Chaldean Oracle, Anonymous

Deriving our sense of self from experience is, we saw, like describing a hole in a piece of wood in terms of the qualities of the wood rather than those of the hole itself. Our true nature, like the air that fills the hole, is far less tangible than the derived self, yet it is the one element common to all experience.

The search for this underlying self—what might be called our real essence—has engrossed the attention of people the world over for thousands of years. The eighteenth-century Scottish philosopher David Hume, for example, repeatedly looked within himself in an attempt to discover something he could call his true self. Yet he found that "when I enter most intimately into what I call *myself,* I always stumble on some particular perception or other, of heat or cold, light or shade, love or hatred, pain or pleasure. I never catch *myself* at any time without a perception, and never can observe anything but a perception."

Hume's difficulty is not an unusual one. The self cannot be experienced in the same way that other things are. For us to have any kind of experience two components are necessary. There must be an object of experience, that which is being experienced, whether it be something in the external world, a sensation in the body, a mental image, or a feeling; and there must be a subject of experience, an experiencer, that which is having the experience. It was this subject of experience that Hume was looking for in his search for the self.

Yet to be able to experience the self in the same way that anything else is experienced would require that the self become an object of experience. This is essentially why such an approach fails to find anything. It is rather like entering a room where the only light comes from a flash-light on one's head, then proceeding to search for the source of the light. All that one sees are various objects, reflecting the light.

This is not to say that the subject of all experience is completely unknowable, only that this Self (with a capital S to distinguish it from the derived self of Chapter 11) can-not be experienced in the same way that anything else can be experienced, for it is itself the experiencer. It is not an experience of "I am this or that", but rather the "I who experience this or that".

Thus whatever we may think or perceive ourselves to be is not the pure Self, the subject of all experience, the *I* that is thinking and perceiving, but some aspect of our ex-perience. As a result we come to identify with the contents of our awareness, with our experience, rather than with the true Self.

To identify means literally "to make the same" (from the Latin *idem-ficare*). What we identify with is what we make the same as I, yet the very fact that we have to *make* those things the same as I, implies they are not really I to begin with. You can see this for yourself by taking an aspect of yourself that you feel is intrinsically you and asking if the feeling of I-ness would be different if that aspect were dif-ferent. You might start by asking if the feeling of I-ness would be different if you were three inches taller or if you were of a different race or if you were the opposite sex or if your body was in any way different. You would certainly appear different, but the very fact that *you* could have different physical characteristics shows that the *you* who has those characteristics has not changed. You have a body, yes, you dwell within a body, but *you*—your intrinsic Self, that which in your own experience you label "I"—is more than your body.

The same applies to your emotions. One day you may feel one thing; the next day you may feel something different. Again the intrinsic sense of I-ness has not changed; it is the emotions you experience that have changed. You have emotions, but *you* are not your emotions.

The same is also true of thoughts and desires. You have thoughts, but *you* are not your thoughts. You have desires, but *you* are not your desires.

What then is the nature of the pure Self? What is the essence of this I-ness?

THE PURE SELF

We have seen that for the Self to experience the Self, the experiencer would have to become the object of experience. In this situation, there would no longer be any distinction between the subject and the object and no room for any interaction between them. Experience, as we normally know it, would cease. This would be a state of pure consciousness, devoid of all content.

How are we to understand a state in which there is nothing to be conscious of and yet consciousness itself remains? A good analogy might be the distinction between hearing and listening. Wherever you are, if you listen you will usually hear various sounds around you. But suppose you were in a completely silent room. You could still listen, but there would be nothing to be heard. Likewise, in a state of complete mental silence, you, the experiencer, are conscious, but there is nothing to be conscious of. You are—but you are not any thing.

Since there is no content to this state of consciousness, there is no means by which a person might distinguish his or her most intimate appreciation of I-ness from anyone else's. One is, in effect, in touch with a universal level of the self. If there is any identity at all in this state, it is of an at-one-ness with humanity and the whole of creation.

For most people such a state of consciousness occurs rarely, if ever. Generally, our attention is directed outward, into the world of sensory experience, away from the pure Self. Even when the attention is directed inward, it is usually preoccupied with thoughts of one kind or another. To not have a thought in one's head, not even the idea, "I do not have a thought in my head," is a very rare thing.

Although not part of most people's common experience, there is abundant testimony that this Self-awareness is possible. Descriptions of such states crop up again and again in the writings of mystics and religious teachers around the world and from all periods of history. Yet because the pure Self has none of the usual properties attributable to an experience, it becomes very difficult to describe in words. Indeed, the very act of describing it makes it an object rather than the subject of experience. This is why many mystics speak of it as the ineffable, that of which one cannot speak. It lies beyond descriptions, beyond any idea we might have, and attempts to describe it inevitably make it an idea of some kind.

The *Mundaka Upanishad*, an ancient Indian spiritual text concerned with the nature of the pure Self, sums up this difficulty as follows:

> *It is not outer awareness*
> *It is not inner awareness,*
> *Nor is it a suspension of awareness.*
> *It is not knowing,*
> *It is not unknowing,*
> *Nor is it knowingness itself.*
> *It can neither be seen nor understood,*
> *It cannot be given boundaries.*
> *It is ineffable and beyond thought.*
> *It is indefinable.*
> *It is known only through becoming it.*

In a similar vein, the ancient Chinese text the *Tao Te Ching*, speaking of the absolute nature of all things (the Tao), opens with: "The Tao that can be told is not the eternal Tao."

Yet it will not be of much value to remain completely silent about the nature of this Self. So, bearing in mind these difficulties, let us look at how some of the mystics, those engaged in a personal quest for union with the divine or sacred, have referred to this state, and look in particular at the way in which it has led them to an immediate awareness of their oneness with the whole of creation.

Chuang-Tzu, a Chinese mystic living in the fourth century B.C., wrote quite simply that in this state: "I and all things in the universe are one."

Plotinus, the third-century Egyptian philosopher, said: "Man as he now is has ceased to be the All. But when he ceases to be an individual, he raises himself again and penetrates the whole world."

Meister Eckhart, the thirteenth-century Christian mystic, notes his experience that: "All that man has here externally in multiplicity is intrinsically One. Here all blades of grass, wood and stone, all things are One. This is the deepest depth. . . . "

And Henry Suso, a German Dominican, wrote: "All creatures. . . are the same life, the same essence, the same power, the same one and nothing less."

What these mystics seem to be saying is that at the deepest level of my being, I am of the same essence as you and the same as the rest of the universe. We are all of this same essence, and I experience my Self as such. This is what we are the same as, this is our deepest level of identity.

For most of us, accustomed to thinking of ourselves as completely separate individuals, this may indeed be a very difficult concept to grasp. An analogy used by several different spiritual teachers might help make the idea clearer. Our individual consciousnesses are like drops of water taken from an ocean: each drop is unique, with its own particular qualities and identity; yet each drop is also of the same essence as the ocean.

THE PERENNIAL PHILOSOPHY

This experience of unity can be seen to form the core of all mystical and religious traditions. On the surface, the various religions might appear to offer very different teachings about the nature of reality and the means toward achieving salvation or liberation. But once one begins to pare away the cultural trappings and the additions and corrections imposed by later commentators and translators, a basic teaching begins to emerge which is common to them: we are, at our cores, united.

The writer and novelist Aldous Huxley, who studied the major religious and mystical traditions in considerable depth, called this basic teaching The Perennial Philosophy. It is, in Huxley's words, that which "recognizes a divine Reality substantial to the world of things and lives and minds; the psychology that finds in the soul something similar to, or even identical with, divine Reality; the ethic that places man's final end in the knowledge of the immanent and transcendent Ground of all being."

The Upanishads, for example, tell us that:

> *What is within us is also without.*
> *What is without us is also within.*

Remarkably similar is this statement from the recently discovered Gospel according to Thomas: "The Kingdom is within you and it is without you." And *The Awakening of Faith*, an early Buddhist treatise written by Ashvaghosha, expresses that: "All things from the beginning are in their nature Being itself."

An important point to note about the perennial philosophy is that it is not a philosophy in the Western sense,
for it is not an ideology or belief system. Rather, it is based
on the experiences of those who have tasted such states. It
is not so much a set of ideas to be thought about or debated
as an invitation to turn within and discover these truths for
oneself. The consequent changes in awareness, life-style,
and morality may be profound, but they come as a result of
knowing this state of pure *being*, rather than through the
acceptance of any conceptual system or doctrine.

Moreover, the perennial philosophy repeatedly declares
that the realization of our essential oneness is not reserved
for a select few. Because the Self is common to everyone,
we all have the potential to be aware of our real inner na
tures. Thus we find similar descriptions among writers,
such as the poet Tennyson, who wrote in a letter to a friend:
"Individuality itself seemed to dissolve and fade away into
boundless being, and this was not a confused state but the
clearest, the surest of the sure, utterly beyond words—where
death was almost a laughable impossibility—the loss of
personality (if so it were) seeming no extinction but the
only true life."

Edward Carpentier, the nineteenth-century social scientist and poet, wrote:

If you inhibit thought (and persevere) you come
at length to a region of consciousness below or
behind thought. . . and a realization of an altogether vaster self than that to which we are
accustomed. And since the ordinary consciousness, with which we are concerned in daily life, is

before all things founded on the little local self. . .
it follows that to pass out of that is to die to the
ordinary self and the ordinary world.

It is to die in the ordinary sense, but in another, it
is to wake up and find that the "I," one's real, most
intimate self, pervades the Universe and all other
things—that the mountains and the sea and the
stars are a part of one's body and that one's soul is
in touch with the souls of all creatures.

CHAPTER 14

AWAKENING THE SELF

A human being is part of the whole, called by us "Universe," a part limited in time and space. He experiences himself, his thoughts and feelings as something separated from the rest—a kind of optical delusion of his consciousness. This delusion is a kind of prison for us, restricting us to our personal desires and to affection for a few persons nearest to us

Our task must be to free ourselves from this prison by widening our circle of compassion to embrace all living creatures and the whole of nature in its beauty.

Albert Einstein

The perennial philosophy repeatedly affirms that we are all ultimately one. It further suggests that this oneness is knowable as the pure Self at the very core of our being, and that this realization is open to all—indeed, it is our birthright. Yet the vast majority of people do not live in such a state of consciousness. Perhaps this is because we have all been conditioned—some would say hypnotized—by our upbringing and culture to see only the superficial side of our identity. The pure, universal Self, is ever present, but most of us are asleep to it. As the eighteenth-century English poet, painter, and visionary William Blake wrote in the *Marriage of Heaven and Hell:*

> *If the doors of perception were cleansed,*
> *everything would appear to man as it is, infinite.*
>
> *For man has closed himself up, 'till he sees all*
> *things thro' narrow chinks in his cavern.*

As an analogy, let us return for a moment to the example of the black and white patches on page 168. With appropriate visual clues, it became possible to see them as a picture of a man's face, and once having seen the face, it was usually obvious that the face was, in a sense, always there. Without a shift in set, however, it could not be seen at all—"What is he talking about? A face in there?"

It seems to be the same with the pure Self. The reality of the self as a universal Self may be there, obvious to those who know it, but if we have not made the necessary shift in set we simply cannot see it. This is what the Zen Buddhist masters mean when they say, "You are already enlightened; all you have to do is wake up to the fact."

The question is: How do we wake up? How do we dehypnotize ourselves? Answering this question could very well be one of the most crucial tasks facing humanity today.

It is not sufficient to know *intellectually* that we are inseparable from the rest of the universe, if reality is still perceived dualistically as "I am in here" and the rest of the world is "out there".

For humanity to accomplish a profound shift in attitude, the skin-encapsulated self needs to be augmented by the realization that the individual is an integral part of nature, no more isolated from the environment than a cell in the body is isolated from the human organism. The word *realization* (i.e., to make real) is crucial, for a truly holistic ecological ethic cannot be built into our attitudes, policies, and actions unless it is first built into ourselves. It needs to be an immediately experienced fact of life, an unavoidable premise of all our thoughts, perceptions, feelings, and actions. We need to realize our essential oneness with nature, not just with our intellect and reason but with our feelings and with our souls. It must become an undeniable part of our reality.

From what we have already seen of the egocentric model, it might appear very difficult to make such a shift. This model has been built up from early infancy; it is one of our strongest conditionings. It is further reinforced by language, social institutions, and the behavior of those around us. Moreover, a self-model cannot be changed by thinking, by argument, by analysis, or by simply deciding to change it. It is the frame of reference that underlies all thought, argument, analysis, and decision making, and as such is beyond their scope.

As we saw earlier, our self-model conditions all our

mental activity, and in this respect may be considered as a metaparadigm, similar to a scientific paradigm, but pervading all areas of thinking. Scientific paradigms are likewise very resistant to change; yet change they do. We might therefore find some clues as to how to initiate a shift in metaparadigm—that is, in our self-model—by looking in more detail at how parallel shifts occur in science.

THE COPERNICAN REVOLUTION

As we saw earlier, a classic example of a paradigm shift was the Copernican revolution in astronomy. The old paradigm of the earth at the center of the universe, with the moon, sun, planets, and stars revolving around it, had been formulated by the Greek astronomer Ptolemy around 140 A.D. This paradigm was based on Plato's belief that circular motion was the perfect motion. Heavenly bodies, it was held, displayed perfect motion and must therefore move around the earth in circles.

Observation showed, however, that the planets did not move in smooth circles around the earth; their speed varied, and sometimes they even reversed their motions. Ptolemy managed to account for these anomalies by suggesting that the planets moved round smaller circles whose centers moved round the earth in circular orbits. This produces a curve known as an epicycle, which approximated the path of the planets and allowed the principle of circular motion to be retained.

As measurements became accurate, more anomalies were discovered, and these were accounted for by the addition of more complex epicycles and the introduction of various oscillations until the system became very complex indeed. This model, cumbersome as it was, survived unchallenged for thirteen hundred years.

Over the centuries a few brave souls had suggested that the sun, not the earth, lay at the center of the system. This theory had even been put forward by some of the early Greek astronomers but had received little recognition. It was only in the sixteenth century that Nicholas Copernicus attracted more attention to the idea by giving it a clear mathematical formulation. He showed that if the sun lay at the center, many of the anomalous motions of the planets could be explained at one stroke. Copernicus, however, still adhered to Plato's idea of perfect circular motion and still tried to account for irregularities in terms of epicycles.

The suggestion that the earth did not lie at the center of the universe was heresy to the Church, and Copernicus withheld publication of his work. His fears were well founded. Some of his supporters were punished by the Church, some even burnt at the stake. And when his own work was eventually published—Copernicus received a copy on the last day of his life—it was placed on the papal index of forbidden books.

The next step toward a new paradigm came eighty years later when Johannes Kepler, a German astronomer, had the good fortune to come into possession of volumes of extraordinarily accurate astronomical observations made by the Danish astronomer Tycho Brahe. Working on this data, Kepler came to the realization that the sun-centered system could explain the various motions, without any need for complex "epicycling", provided that the planets traveled in ellipses rather than circles.

These two major shifts—the shift away from the idea
of earth being at the center of the universe and the shift
away from circular motion—together gave birth to a new
paradigm, a radically different world view.

Yet even though the model worked very satisfactorily,
it was still not readily accepted by the establishment. When,
for example, in the early 1600s, the Italian mathematician
Galileo, using the new invention of the telescope, gath-

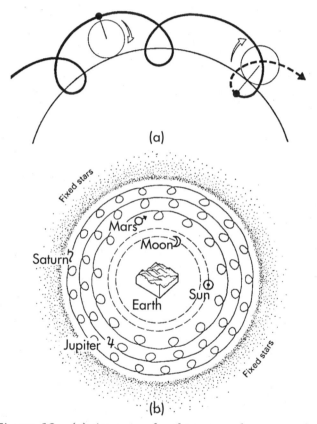

Figure 12. (a) An epicycle: the curve drawn out by a
point attached to a circle that is rolling around a second
circle. (b) The Ptolemaean view of the universe with
the planets moving around the Earth on epicycles.

ered evidence to support Kepler's model, the professors in the universities felt very threatened. They united against Galileo and denounced him to the Church for blasphemy. He was hauled before the Inquisition, where he was forced to "abjure, curse, and detest" the absurd view that the Earth moves around the sun.

It was not until Sir Isaac Newton published his major work, the *Principia*, in 1687, that the new model was finally accepted. Newton laid down the basic laws of gravitation, which provided the theoretical underpinning for Kepler's theories. The paradigm shift was now complete.

Looking at the general patterns that characterize this and many other equally significant paradigm shifts, science historians such as Thomas Kuhn have shown that such changes seem to go through the following stages:

1. Anomalous findings that cannot be explained away in terms of the currently accepted paradigm. Initially these anomalies may be rejected as spurious or fallacious, or the model may be "stretched" to incorporate them.

2. An increase in the number of such anomalies until they can no longer be so easily discounted or accommodated, and it is realized that the paradigm may be at fault rather than the observations.

3. The formulation of a new paradigm that explains the new findings.

4. A transition in which the new paradigm is challenged by the establishment, sometimes leading to bitter struggles by those who are attached to the old paradigm.

5. Acceptance of the new paradigm as it explains further observations and predicts new findings.

The Identity Shift

Like a scientific paradigm, the skin-encapsulated model of the self gains status through its ability to provide a coherent framework for experience. This status is reinforced by the fact that most of what happens to us can be understood through the model of "I am in here" and the world is "out there". Every perception of the outside world can be fitted into the egocentric model, precisely because it is an experience of the outside world. As far as normal experience is concerned, therefore, there would seem to be no anomalous phenomena that might threaten the model.

Even the impending global catastrophe, which has its roots in the dualist self-model, is still perceived by the I "in here". Today's crises are crises only for the social, economic, technological, and political paradigms; they make us intellectually aware that something is wrong with our world view, but they do not directly challenge our experience of the skin-encapsulated self. Consequently we tend to ask what we can do about the world rather than what we can do about ourselves, and the self-model remains unquestioned.

The one phenomenon that directly challenges that skin-encapsulated model is the personal experience of unboundedness, of oneness with the rest of creation, the immediate awareness that *I* and everything else are, at their most fundamental levels, of one essence. This direct personal experience of unity is the anomalous observation that cannot be incorporated within the skin-encapsulated model. This is the crisis for the old identity, revealing the model's incompleteness and starting the shift toward a new self-model.

In the case of a scientific paradigm, one single anomalous observation does not by itself produce a major shift; it is usually either ignored or explained away. The same is likely to occur with shifts in identity. There are many instances of people who have at times tasted such states of unity, when suddenly they perceive themselves and the world as a single whole. These states of consciousness may be brought on by a beautiful sunset, long-distance running, meditation, drugs, intense emotion, the view of planet Earth from space, or seemingly by nothing in particular.

But it is one thing to have had such experiences; it is quite another thing to have this awareness of unity become the fundamental basis of all perception, thinking, and action. Most people who experience such unitary states find that afterwards they return to the dualist, skin-encapsulated model of the self. The memory of having experienced an intimate oneness with creation may well remain, but the oneness itself is no longer an inescapable reality. From the standpoint of the old self such experiences may, like the anomalies in a scientific paradigm, be cast off as mental aberrations, hallucinations, or some strange quirk in brain function.

For a true shift in identity to begin, the anomalies must build up until a point is reached where the old, egocentric identity is no longer tenable and begins to lose its status. Thus the experience of oneness usually needs to be repeated again and again before it can begin to be included as part of one's personal reality. The identity has to be reconditioned to unity. This, as we shall see in Chapter 16, is the purpose of many spiritual disciplines and practices of meditation. They are processes through which one can come to know this other reality and partake of this awareness repeatedly.

THE NEW COPERNICAN REVOLUTION

In the case of paradigm shifts, one of two things can happen to the old model. It can be rejected as erroneous, as was the case with the Copernican revolution. Alternatively, the old model can be incorporated within the new model. This is what happened with Einstein's revolution in physics, where Newton's laws of motion were retained as a special case of the theory of relativity.

It is this second type of shift that is needed with our model of the self. It will not be necessary to reject the skin-encapsulated model, because the sense of individual uniqueness and separateness has important value in terms of our biological identity and autonomy. The problematic behavior that we looked at earlier stems, not from this ego-centric model of the self, but from our dependence on this as the *only* form of self. The shift in identity should therefore be one that could accommodate the skin-encapsulated model as a valuable, but partial, view of the self.

Willis Harman, president of The Institute of Noetic Sciences—an organization founded by the astronaut Edgar Mitchell in order to investigate untapped potentials of the human mind—has referred to this shift of consciousness as the *new* Copernican revolution. In the original Copernican revolution, the geocentric model of the physical universe was turned inside out. The earth lost its position at the center of the universe; the sun became the center with the earth revolving around it. In the new Copernican revolution, our egocentric model of the material world would be similarly inverted. The individual ego, which for so long has been assumed to be the center of our inner universe, would be put in its proper position, that is, revolving around the pure Self, the true center of all consciousness, what T.S. Eliot referred to as the "still point of the turning world".

The original Copernican revolution came about by gaining greater knowledge of the whole system, not by changing the movement of the earth nor by trying to make the sun stand still. So the new Copernican revolution will come about by expanding our awareness of our own inner natures, not by trying to destroy or restrain the ego or by trying to hold onto an idea of the pure Self. To try to destroy individual identity, or to think as if one were at one with the rest of creation, without first gaining a personal experience of the fact, would only create dissonance between theory and experience. Moreover, a strong sense of an individual self is probably essential for social interaction, communication, and self-improvement. To destroy the ego would be to take away the motor of our world.

ENLIGHTENMENT

The state in which the pure Self has become a permanently established reality is what many spiritual traditions refer to as self-realization or enlightenment. Used in this sense, enlightenment means more than being particularly wise, aware, or well balanced; it denotes a clearly defined state of consciousness. The enlightened person is still functioning as an individual organism, preserving a sense of biological autonomy. And to this awareness of individuality is now added the equally real awareness of unity with the rest of creation. Oneness and separateness become two different perspectives of identity.

The important point about the enlightened state of consciousness is that the individual is no longer dependent upon the environment for his sense of personal existence, since the pure Self is not affected by the ups and downs of the outside world. Thus the incessant need to repair an injured ego, to reassert it whenever some threat arises, no longer exists. Indeed, to reaffirm the ego at the expense of others and the world around would now be in direct conflict with the experience of oneness with the external world.

The fact that the enlightened person no longer needs to derive a sense of self from his interactions with the external world does not mean that he is devoid of personality, character, or idiosyncrasies. In these respects enlightened people are as individual as anybody else (as any survey of enlightened mystics and religious teachers will instantly show). What is important is that they are no longer psychologically attached to these attributes. It is in this sense that they are "egoless". It is not that they have lost their individual egos; it is that they have lost the continual need to reaffirm them. Action ceases to be dominated by the ego and becomes more appropriate to the situation at hand.

Since he is no longer psychologically dependent on his experience, the enlightened person is not kicked around by the world. Personal criticism, loss of a job, or other events that before would have been a source of anguish are still very real, but they are no longer perceived as personal threats. This is borne out by the experience of many people who, though not enlightened, are nevertheless already making progress in this direction. They often remark that it is not so much the sense of oneness that first becomes noticeable but the experience of being at ease with themselves, combined with an increasing sense of inner security and invulnerability.

OPENING OF THE HEART

With this liberation from the needs of the derived self comes a simultaneous opening of the heart. Love, which before was conditional (conditional upon the person finding another person in some way lovable) now becomes less conditional. The enlightened person begins to experience a spontaneous love for every creature and every thing, whatever their qualities or attributes.

The growth of such a love is a recurrent theme in most religions. It is, for example, a principal aspect of the Christian tradition. The Greek word *caritas*, sometimes translated in the gospels as charity, originally meant dearness or closeness, love in the sense of an at-one-ness. This is love in a much deeper and far-reaching sense than just friendliness or looking after one's neighbor. We may take the phrase "love thy neighbor as thyself" as an injunction to feel and act in a certain way. But it was probably never meant as an injunction at all. It is not an attitude we must try to have but a state of consciousness we need to reach, the state in which you know your neighbor (and everybody else) to be of the same essence as thy self.

For most of us, the experience of true affinity seldom encompasses more than a few other individuals. Rather than feeling an affinity for the rest of the world, most people feel alienated from it. A genuine love for the rest of creation comes from the personal experience of oneness with the rest of creation, the awareness that, at the deepest level, the self and the world are one. A deep affinity with everyone and everything then arises quite spontaneously, as a natural consequence of being in this state of consciousness.

We find the same message stated very succinctly in the ancient Chinese *Tao Te Ching:* "Love the world as your own self; then you can truly care for all things."

Twenty-five hundred years later, Teilhard de Chardin, elaborating on this theme, wrote in *The Future of Man:* "It is not a *tête-a-tête* or a *corps-a-corps* that we need; it is a heart-to-heart. . . . If the synthesis of the Spirit is to be brought about in entirety (and this is the only possible definition of progress), it can only be done, in the last resort, through the meeting, *center to center,* of human units, such as can only be realized in the universal, mutual love."

He goes on to add that "there is but one possible way in which human elements, innumerably diverse by nature, can love one another: it is by knowing themselves all to be centered on a single 'supercenter' common to all."

The enlightened person experiences a deep and universal compassion, and his life usually becomes one of service, not just service to humanity but to the whole world. In the words of a Buddhist scripture, "The fair tree of thought that knows no duality bears the flower and fruit of compassion, and its name is service of others."

The enlightened person knows a reality that lies beyond the everyday duality of "I" and "not I" and the suffering it causes, and his compassion for humanity makes him want to help others to achieve this realization as well. For this reason many Buddhist teachings have proclaimed that the enlightened being does not rest till he has seen the enlightenment of all beings.

It is toward this goal of universal enlightenment that humanity needs to move. Those who have achieved enlightenment have generally been few and far between. But, if the world is to be transformed and a high synergy society is to become a reality, such a shift in consciousness will need to be widespread.

CHAPTER 15

HEALING THE PLANETARY CANCER

> Dark and cold we may be, but this
> Is no winter now. The frozen misery
> Of centuries breaks, cracks, begins to move;
> The thunder is the thunder of the floes,
> The thaw, the flood, the upstart Spring.
> Thank God our time is now when wrong
> Comes up to face us everywhere,
> Never to leave us 'til we take
> The longest stride of soul men ever took.
> *Christopher Fry*

A worldwide shift toward a higher state of consciousness has important implications for the hypothesis
that human society is like a planetary cancer. We saw in
Chapter 3 that there were a number of parallels between
the way a malignant growth develops in the human being,

eventually destroying the body on which it is ultimately dependent, and the way in which humanity appears to be eating its way indiscriminately across the surface of the planet, disrupting and possibly destroying its planetary host. In malignant tissue the individual cells cease to function as a part of a larger organism. They feed and reproduce themselves at the expense of the rest of the body. They are in a sense egocentric cells. Cancer is, in this respect, a low-synergy phenomenon.

The synergy of a living organism depends upon the DNA molecules in the nucleus of each of its cells. The precise arrangement of numerous smaller molecules along any particular strand of DNA gives rise to a particular genetic code. Different people carry slightly different genetic codes on the DNA, but within any particular individual that same genetic information is contained in virtually every single cell. The coding determines not only the way in which every single cell functions, it also provides an essential element of common programming, which links the individual cell to the organism as a whole.

The reason why a particular cell becomes cancerous is that this genetic program is in some way disturbed or interfered with. This can happen in several ways. It may be caused by the effect of toxic chemicals, by exposure to X-rays or nuclear radiation, or simply because, in the process of constantly regenerating its billions of cells, the body occasionally makes an imperfect one. In the healthy organism the odd imperfection is quickly dealt with, but in the weak or stressed organism the cell may survive. But since its programming is disturbed it no longer functions in harmony with the whole. It becomes what is termed a rogue cell, functioning in a low-synergy manner. It may also start producing other cells in which the genetic code is similarly disturbed, leading to a malignant growth.

A MALIGNANT SOCIETY

At the level of society, that which ties the individual back to the system, and performs the function parallel to our genetic programs, are our beliefs—the programs in our own minds. If these programs are in alignment with the needs of others and our surroundings, then the synergy of society will be high. But generally they are not. Too often our attitudes and values are driven by the needs of our derived sense of self. And since the survival of such an identity is continually at stake, a whole set of self-survival programs are triggered—fear, aggression, hoarding, seeing others as threats rather than allies. Such behaviors might be appropriate if our physical survival were threatened, but not when it is only the survival of the illusory ego that is threatened. In these circumstances they lead to low synergy and malignant behavior towards others and our environment.

It may well be that human cancer and the planetary cancer are even more closely related than this analogy suggests; they may be two different symptoms of the same problem. Human cancer has steadily become more prevalent in the last few decades, particularly in the more developed Western nations, at the same time that those nations have become more malignant in their approach to the environment. Some of the increase may be due, paradoxically, to better health care; when tuberculosis was a major killer, not so many people had the chance to go on to develop cancer.

Modern life-styles are also a major element. Contemporary diets have been implicated, as have general attitudes toward life. We are also finding that numerous products (e.g., hair dyes, suntan oils, asbestos fibers, photocopying fluids, and chlorinated drinking water), not to mention numerous airborne pollutants and radioactivity, may be cancer inducing. These are all examples that stem from the low synergy of contemporary society, and which in turn lead to low synergy and cancer in the individual.

In order to reverse this malignant trend in society we need to be tied back once again to the system as a whole through an experience of our oneness within the world. Interestingly, the Latin word for "to tie again" is *re-ligare,* and the word *religion* originally meant just this: that which ties us again to our common source.

This does not mean to imply that we need to return to conventional religion, for, as the next chapter will show, conventional religion has generally lost the art of religare. What we do need is a spiritual renewal, a widespread shift in consciousness along the lines experienced by the great mystics and proponents of the perennial philosophy.

Such a shift has now become supremely important, not only for the well-being of the individuals and society as a whole, but also for Gaia herself; it is the path to a spontaneous global remission. In this respect the person whose goal is self-realization, whether he be a yogi in a Himalayan cave or an office worker in Los Angeles, is helping to change the world at the most fundamental level. Such people are perhaps the ultimate revolutionaries.

EVOLUTION FROM THE INSIDE

We have seen that the shift from an ego-dominated model of the self to a more universal model seems to be a very necessary ingredient in the development of a higher synergy and in the transformation of humanity into a healthy social superorganism. In this respect the development of self-realization is supporting the general thrust of evolution toward the progressive integration of the human species.

We can, however, go further than this. We can see the development of higher states of consciousness to be an essential part of the evolutionary process itself.

The previous evolutionary leap to self-reflective consciousness not only allowed us to be aware of ourselves as conscious, thinking beings, but also gave us the capacity to be conscious of the essence of consciousness itself, the pure Self. It thereby bestowed upon us the possibility of becoming spiritually enlightened.

Moreover, with the emergence of self-reflective consciousness the platform of evolution moved up from life to consciousness. Consciousness became the spearhead of evolution. For the first time on Earth evolution became internalized. Thus the urge that many people feel to grow and develop inwardly may well be the force of evolution manifesting itself within our own consciousnesses. It is the universe evolving through us.

This inner evolution is not an aside to the overall process of evolution. Conscious inner evolution is the particular phase of evolution that we, in our corner of the universe, are currently passing through.

From this perspective the movement toward a social superorganism and the mystical urge to know an inner unity are complementary aspects of the same single process, the thrust of evolution toward higher degrees of wholeness. To flow with evolution is, therefore, to explore our own inner selves and find unity and wholeness within.

The question now facing humanity is: How can we facilitate this inner evolution, and, even more important, can we do it in time?

CHAPTER 16

A SPIRITUAL RENAISSANCE

When the Tao is lost, there is goodness.
When goodness is lost, there is kindness.
When kindness is lost, there is justice.
When justice is lost, there is ritual.
Now ritual is the husk of faith and loyalty,
and the beginning of confusion.

Tao Te Ching, 6th Century B.C.

The experience of unity with the whole of creation, in addition to being closely connected with spiritual and religious traditions, is also an experience that has received considerable attention from a number of psychologists.

Some of the first psychologists to look seriously at religious experience were William James and Carl Jung, followed in the 1950s by Abraham Maslow and Roberto Assagioli. Out of this work, a new school of psychology—

transpersonal psychology—developed in the late 1960s; its main focus has been the study of religious and related experiences. Previously, psychotherapy had been preoccupied with treating people with mental or emotional problems. But some psychology professionals such as Maslow turned away from the study of the sick to look at the mentally healthy, and at the exceptionally healthy in particular. Maslow found that such people had a high incidence of what he called "peak experiences", states in which they felt "at one with the world, really belonging to it, instead of being outside looking in. . . the feeling that they had really seen the ultimate truth." They had a "sense of unity of everything, and of the universe itself being alive." In this respect such experiences sound very much like glimpses of the unitive Self.

Maslow observed that these people were composed, stable, and integrated members of society. They also displayed a characteristic he termed "self-actualization", "the actualization of potential, capacities, and talents, as fulfillment of mission, as a fuller knowledge of and acceptance of the person's own intrinsic nature, as an unceasing trend toward unity, integration or synergy. . . ." Most importantly, Maslow found that self-actualizers tended to be centered on problems external to themselves rather than ego-maintenance. They had a strong sense of identity with humanity as a whole and a feeling of belonging to something bigger, even the whole of creation. From such descriptions it would seem that these people were probably moving along the path toward what we have called enlightenment.

A study by two American sociologists, Adam Greeley and William McCready, reported in *The New York Times*

Magazine, showed that peak experiences are far from uncommon. Forty-three percent of the people they
interviewed had had an experience of going beyond their
normal self, 20 percent on more than one occasion. Most
of those interviewed had never spoken of their experience
to anyone before, generally because they were afraid that
they might be laughed at. Yet the fact that so many people
had such experiences would suggest that many of the people
in whom they might have confided would have had similar
experiences themselves.

Common to many experiences were feelings of joy and
happiness, an inability to describe the experience in words,
an awareness of the unity in everything, and a realization
that this is the way things really are—again, all characteristic of the unitive Self. Moreover, as with Maslow's work,
Greely and McCready found a strong relationship between
these experiences and psychological well-being.

Studies such as these go a long way toward supporting
the perennial philosophy's claim that such states can be
known by anyone, that they are not the prerogative of a
select few. However, it is one thing to have tasted such
experiences; it is quite another to have had them so frequently that they become the dominant mode of
consciousness. This brings us to the question of what, if
anything, can we do to facilitate these experiences and make
them much more commonplace?

Perhaps our first thought would be to look to conventional religion. In all, there are dozens of different religions
of the world, and many times that number of sects (Buddhism alone contains over six hundred different sects). Yet,
separate and unique as each religion might appear to be, it

is possible to see a common theme underlying them all. Walter Stace, who was a professor of philosophy at Princeton, studied at length the writings and teachings of the great religious teachers and came to the conclusion that the central core of all the major religions was the experience of oneness with creation—what Huxley called the perennial philosophy.

Each particular tradition originally arose from the teachings of individuals—Christ, Buddha, Moses, Mohammed, Mani, Zoroaster, Guru Nanak, Shankara, Lao Tse—and a close examination of what they said, or were reported to have said, suggests that they were each in their own terms referring to this basic unitary experience. Christ may have spoken of the Kingdom of Heaven, Buddha of *Nirvana* ("deliverance"), and Shankara of *Moksha* ("liberation"), but in doing so they each appear to have been describing aspects of enlightenment. Moreover, if one looks at the practices they taught, such as prayer, meditation, devotion, abstention, dancing, or prostration, they each appear to have been giving prescriptions whereby the ordinary person could come closer to that state.

Once the teacher was gone, however, his teachings began to suffer distortion. This is inevitable; it is the equivalent of entropy in the field of knowledge—or what I sometimes call "truth decay". Each time a message is passed on from one person to another there is some slight change; something may be inadvertently omitted or some little extra thing included. Unintentionally, but unavoidably, the original spiritual teachings lose their purity as they pass down through history. The medium destroys the message.

As far as the theoretical aspects of a teaching are concerned, distortion can be minimized by writing down or memorizing the philosophy and doctrine. But the actual techniques and practices are much more delicate and often cannot be put neatly into words. Most spiritual practices require guidance from an experienced teacher, and only a slight distortion or misunderstanding can cause a technique to lose its effectiveness. When this happens adherents to a particular tradition become cut off from the goal of the practice—the state of unity consciousness. The net result is that the means to achieve the experience of oneness are lost much more rapidly than are descriptions of the state.

Conventional religion today reflects the tragedies of this continued differential distortion. Doctrines and dogmas abound, and their adherents argue endlessly over which are the best. Yet without the means to experience the states of consciousness being discussed, true enlightenment remains an unobtainable dream for all but a lucky few. The experience of unity with the whole of creation may have been their aim, but the major religions today do not facilitate this experience; they have become but the fossils of enlightenment.

What humanity urgently needs today are the means to bring about a widespread shift in consciousness. This will come about, not through a revival of any particular religion, but through a revival of the techniques and experiences that once gave these teachings life and effectiveness. We need to rediscover the practices that directly enable the experience of the pure Self and facilitate its permanent integration into our lives.

PATHS OF AWAKENING

Such a revival is already underway. Throughout the Western world there is a rapidly growing number of spiritual masters and gurus teaching different meditation techniques and paths to enlightenment. There are also a growing number of therapies and training programs, all aimed ultimately at bringing about an awareness of the inner Self. Whether or not they are all effective in this respect is a question we shall consider shortly. They are, however, indicative of an increasing trend.

A large number of these practices involve some form of meditation, though the term is used to mean many different types of techniques. Underlying most meditation practices is the basic premise that to contact the underlying Self, the mind must be cleared of its normal clutter of sensory input and endless trains of thought.

Even when sitting quietly doing nothing in particular, most people find there is some internal dialogue occupying their attention to a greater or lesser extent. As a result, they are not aware of the "I" who thinks, only aware of what they are thinking about. Thus a common goal of most meditation techniques is to come to a state of consciousness in which there is no thought: a state of complete mental silence. Since in this state all experience (in the normal sense of the word *experience*) has ceased, only the pure Self, the experiencer, remains.

This is not a blanking out of the mind. It is a common misconception to imagine that one can arrive at this state by deliberately making the mind empty. This effort usually shifts the internal dialogue to the thought that "my mind is blank"—a deceptive and misleading *thought*. In true meditation one leaves verbal thought behind. The internal dialogue, which seems to occupy so much of our waking consciousness, decreases and eventually disappears. To see the various ways in which different meditations set about achieving this, let us look very briefly at some of the more common approaches.

In Transcendental Meditation (TM), one of the simpler and more widespread practices in the West, the person sits down quietly and silently thinks a "mantra," which as far as TM is concerned is just a meaningless sound, although in other types of meditation the mantra may have a specific meaning. In TM one attends to the mantra in a passive manner, not forcing it into any particular form or rhythm. This passive, effortless mode of attention is greatly helped by the fact that the mantra has no meaning; it does not, in itself, lead to a long train of associative thought. As with most meditation techniques, one shifts from an active "doing" mode of attention to a passive "letting be" mode. As a result, the attention is led to experience the normal thinking process at quieter and quieter levels until eventually mental activity fades away completely.

The normal, active mind might be likened to a roomful of people, everyone chattering away to each other. The experience of TM corresponds to everybody's beginning to talk more and more softly until eventually the room falls completely silent. In this state the listener would still be conscious and listening, although nothing would be heard. In a similar way, when the mind becomes completely still, one is nevertheless conscious, although nothing is being thought. One has effectively transcended normal thinking—hence the name Transcendental Meditation.

Most types of Buddhist meditation also start with techniques aimed at helping the mind settle down. In some schools, particularly those of Tibetan Buddhism, this often involves visualization exercises, to take the attention away from verbal thought. Other schools start with breathing exercises, which, in addition to having a settling effect in themselves, also serve as a technique of passive attention, with the rising and falling breath used much like a mantra.

Although the majority of meditation techniques aim at bringing the mind to a state of stillness, some practices take a somewhat different approach. A student practicing more advanced Buddhist techniques, for example, may try to realize the essential Self by progressively disidentifying with the more superficial levels of identity, that is, by realizing one is not one's body, ideas, or feelings. As this process is repeated—uncovering and then disidentifying with subtler and subtler levels of the self—each step takes one nearer to the attributeless, pure Self.

In some Zen Buddhist schools the shift in identity is brought on more dramatically. The master gives the student a *koan*, a paradoxical question or apparently insoluble riddle, such as "What is the sound of one hand clapping?" Such puzzles are impervious to solution by reason alone, although the student may repeatedly return to the master thinking he has worked out the answer. Eventually, after lengthy pondering and in a state of extreme frustration, when his reasoning and discursive faculties have exhausted themselves, he may suddenly break through into *satori* ("a flash of enlightenment"). He has not necessarily found any new interpretations or ideas; rather he has transcended the normal discursive mind and, for a moment, broken through his skin-encapsulated world view.

Such practices are just a few of the many different spiritual approaches to self-realization, and each of those I have mentioned is far more complex than suggested by these very brief descriptions. Even so, the diversity of possible approaches is readily apparent. There are, moreover, many other processes and activities that can have similar effects.

Many people have found the state of inner silence coming through such "physical" disciplines as hatha yoga and t'ai chi. Some experience it through long-distance running or various other forms of prolonged physical exertion. Some have reached this state through fasting, through pain or suffering, through drugs that modify the brain's functioning, through hypnosis and biofeedback, or through sexual experiences. Yet whatever the path, and however deliberate or accidental the breakthrough, the result is nearly always the same: a transcendence of the skin-encapsulated ego and an opening to a deeper, unifying self.

OBSTACLES ON THE PATH

Despite this diversity of practices and opportunities, true enlightenment remains a rarity. Why is this?

One reason may be the general level of consciousness of society as a whole (something we shall be looking at in Chapter 18). A second reason may be that few of the practices are as effective as they might be. The causes for this are various. The techniques may be difficult to teach correctly, or too easily distorted by the student. Some approaches may require the development of considerable skill before they work. In many cases it may be some time before people notice any change in themselves, and lacking this feedback they may throw the practice away; in other cases they may occasionally have clear experiences of higher states of consciousness, motivating them to keep on, but the experiences may not be frequent enough to produce a permanent shift in consciousness. Certain programs may require a high degree of personal instruction and consultation with a teacher, and there may not be a sufficient number of such teachers available. The approaches derived from the East are sometimes incompatible with everyday Western life-styles. Frequently, the beneficial effects of a particular technique are negated by other influences in a person's life—use of alcohol or other drugs, fatigue, poor health, or stress. And finally, the social environment in which most people live does not usually reinforce any intimations of unity they might have.

If there is one lesson that has been learned since the rush for enlightenment began in the 1960s, it is that enlightenment doesn't follow as rapidly as many of the pundits would have us believe. But this is not necessarily a reason for despondency. As far as the large-scale enlightenment of society is concerned, we are still pioneers—and pioneers make mistakes. (It is, perhaps, worth remembering that the early steam engines that began the Industrial Revolution were not that efficient or successful either.) Yet, as long as the idea of an inner development of consciousness remains alien to externally oriented ways of thinking, it will be easy to scoff at, or even scorn, the trials and errors of the inner explorer.

PSYCHOTECHNOLOGIES

In order for the shift to a higher state of consciousness to become widespread, society will need to develop techniques or processes that are simple to practice, can be incorporated into most people's day-to-day lives, are easily disseminated, and produce the required shifts in consciousness fairly rapidly. Although most of the techniques available today do not sufficiently fulfill these objectives, it is very likely that the contributions of science—psychology and physiology in particular—will ultimately help us to realize these goals.

Just as microscopes, computers, electronic equipment, and a vast array of experimental and analytical techniques have already led to an increased understanding of the outer world, so science and technology are now leading to an increased understanding of the inner world. Electron microscopes, for example, are helping neurophysiologists to examine how individual brain cells function and communicate. Advances in computer analysis and electronics are leading to a better understanding of the extremely complex patterns of electrical activity generated by the combined interaction of the billions of cells in the brain and the ways in which the various regions of the brain interrelate in different states of consciousness. Biochemists are uncovering a wide range of chemical processes that have a direct effect on the brain's functioning and our experience. Other approaches are looking at how different states of consciousness lead to different perceptions of the world around and are studying which factors, both internal and external, trigger changes in consciousness.

As we begin to combine this growing scientific understanding of the brain and consciousness with the knowledge
and techniques of mystics and spiritual teachers, we will
be better able to see how the teachings work, how they can
be improved or developed, and how best to facilitate the
transition from "experimental steam engine" to "mass transportation." With this marriage of East and West will come
the birth of a new discipline, a field aptly called
psychotechnology. More than just the study of the mind or
psyche, it will be the application of techniques to improve
the functioning of the mind and to increase the quality of
experience and the level of consciousness.

Progress in this direction is already being made in a
number of areas. Since the early seventies, a number of scientists have begun to take a serious interest in meditation
and its potential values. During that time more than a thousand research papers were published on the physiological,
psychological, and biochemical effects of meditation. The
general conclusion of these various studies was that meditation produces a physiological state quite opposite to that
of stress; the system becomes very relaxed, and brain activity shows patterns characteristic of a quiet, restful state of
consciousness.

An associated area of research, biofeedback, provides
an excellent example of a dawning psychotechnology. In
this process a person is given information about aspects of
his physiological functioning such as brain rhythms, heart
rate, blood pressure, or skin temperature. This is usually
done by connecting the measuring apparatus to a light or
sound that is switched on whenever the physiological process is in a certain state (e.g., when blood pressure drops

below a certain level). The person is encouraged to make the light or sound come on as much as possible, which he is generally able to do by adopting certain mental attitudes or images. Through such processes a person can learn to control many of the physiological processes that Western physiology had generally thought to be beyond voluntary control.

As the techniques of biofeedback become more sophisticated, and as we come to know in more detail what takes place in the brain during deep meditation and in mystical states of consciousness, it may be possible to use biofeedback to induce or facilitate such states. Considerable progress in this direction has already been made by Dr. James Hardt, of the Biocybernaut Institute in California, one of the early pioneers of biofeedback training. Over the last twenty years he has developed a sophisticated program integrating biofeedback, imagery, and meditation techniques that comes very close to replicating the EEG states found in yogis and zen masters.

Sensory isolation tanks provide another example of the coming together of science and meditation. The purpose of these tanks is to provide an environment in which there is minimal sensory input. Usually the person floats in water at body temperature in a soundproof and lightproof enclosure (hence the term *tank*). Such conditions facilitate the withdrawal of attention from the senses. Many subjects have found that in these environments the inner states characteristic of meditation can be induced more rapidly, and often more deeply.

Hypnosis is another useful tool that has potential for facilitating meditative states of consciousness. Although known about in the West for over a century, hypnosis is still very poorly understood. Nevertheless its profound effects on a person's consciousness are well established. Rather than being just a tool for curious stage effects, or an alternative to anaesthesia in surgery, the principles of hypnosis, when combined with deep relaxation and visualization exercises, are now being seen as powerful means of inducing higher states of consciousness, temporarily shifting a person's identity away from the egocentric model to an awareness of the pure Self. Research in this area is still in its infancy, but it may well prove to be a very powerful tool.

Another possible means for accelerating one's spiritual growth is through the use of psychoactive drugs. For centuries primitive cultures have used extracts from herbs, cacti, mushrooms, vines, and other plants to bring on altered states of consciousness, and since the 1950s a growing number of Westerners have also been experimenting with them. During this same period, chemists have learned to synthesize psychoactive materials, such as psylocibin, mescaline, LSD, MDMA, and DMT. The role of these biochemicals in bringing about religious and mystical states is controversial. Although many people have reported spiritual insights and awakenings from taking such substances, none of our contemporary psychopharmacia appear to bring about a permanent shift to an enlightened state. The experiences and insights may be very valuable, but for real change to occur they need to be integrated into everyday life, which means that spiritual practice of some form or another is still important.

But serious research in this area is still in its infancy.

New designer drugs such as Prozac, Zoloft, and Pexal have shown that it is possible to target particular neurotransmitters in specific areas of the brain and so exercise a high degree of control over mental illnesses such as depression, anxiety, and phobia. Some of these new drugs also seem to lead to beneficial changes in personality. Perhaps in the future other substances will be discovered that trigger the same biochemical states as those associated with enlightenment—and without any undesirable side effects.

These are just a few examples of the ways in which science may be able to further the development of higher states of consciousness. The field is a rapidly expanding one, and within the next decade or so we will probably see psychotechnology become a major area of scientific exploration, bringing with it developments not yet conceived. Moreover, it will probably be one of the most crucial areas of human activity. If as much money, manpower, energy, time, and thought were devoted to the facilitation of higher states of consciousness as are spent on defense—about a trillion dollars a year worldwide—there might no longer be any need to defend ourselves.

In addition to the development of more effective techniques of enlightenment, there is another very important advance in Western technology that will be of immense value in furthering inner transformation: the communications revolution.

In the past there may have been many teachers who have taught practices of self-realization, but these teachers could only directly influence those in their immediate vicinity. Christ imparted his message to those who lived in his area of the Near East, as did Buddha in northern India, but without the technology of mass communication, the knowledge and practices had to be passed on from one person to another. This inevitably led to distortion and a loss of effectiveness. This is one reason why no one has yet succeeded in enlightening humanity as a whole, or even a major part of it.

Today, however, we have a variety of means of communication that can be used to make information available globally. Cars, air travel, postal services, telephones, fax, video and audio recording, satellite links, and computer networks have made it possible to communicate with almost anybody on the world in a variety of different ways. With these developments, it has become possible, for the first time in the history of the planet, to spread the means to self-realization directly and accurately. More important, this possibility has come just at the time when humanity as a whole seems desperately to require a shift into a higher state of consciousness. From an evolutionary perspective, perhaps the ultimate purpose of technology has been to enable society to make this shift.

CHAPTER 17

THE DAWNING OF A NEW ERA

It is precisely the despair of our times that
convinces me that a renaissance is right
around the corner.

Matthew Fox

There is a growing number of people who feel that a
new human era is dawning, one that will involve a
fundamental shift in people's consciousnesses and their relationships to the rest of the planet. Such thinking is often
referred to as the "New Age" movement. The people who
hold these ideas are not united by any central organization;
rather, they constitute a loose and diverse network of groups
united principally by their shared attitudes and values.
Among the recurring themes of the New Age movement
are these: we all have potentials beyond those we are now

using and perhaps others of which we are even unaware; humanity and the environment are a single system; we can improve how we treat ourselves and our surroundings; humanity *can* change for the better.

The New Age movement encompasses a wide and diverse range of interests. There are ecologically oriented groups concerned with the protection of endangered species, organic farming, communal living, alternative technology, voluntary simplicity, energy and resource conservation, nuclear disarmament, and other ways in which we can live more in tune with the planet.

There are people and technologies concerned with improving the health and physiological well-being of the individual through jogging, inner sport, the Alexander technique, the Feldenkrais method, bioenergetics, autogenic training, holistic medicine, acupuncture, spiritual healing, natural childbirth, massage, shiatsu, rolfing, iridology, naturopathy, homeopathy, osteopathy, health foods, whole foods, and dozens of other nutritional diets.

There are numerous methods of therapy, including hypnotherapy, hydrotherapy, dream therapy, art therapy, logotherapy, reality therapy, Reichian therapy, gestalt, primal therapy, and sex therapy, each concerned with improving psychological health and inner well-being. Also oriented in this direction are such treatments as rebirthing, biofeedback, enlightenment intensives, sensitivity training, encounter groups, psychosynthesis, psychodrama, and a plethora of self-development workshops.

There are meditations of numerous kinds drawn from just about every spiritual tradition, as well as practices such as t'ai chi, aikido, tantra, and hatha yoga.

There are groups pursuing the development of "paranormal" abilities such as aura reading, telepathy, and past-life experiences, and various forms of divination from astrology and tarot to geomancy and radionics.

In addition, many others are concerned with such areas as holistic education, feminism, community, and other ways of allowing people to unfold their full potential.

Many of these groups herald the dawning of a new age, not in the far distant future, but in the present time. Some find support for this idea in the number of groups available and the rate at which the interest is spreading—an aspect we shall explore in more detail in the following chapter. Others cite the astrologer's claim that our planet is moving into a new era, the so-called Age of Aquarius.

THE AGE OF AQUARIUS

Astrology divides the sky up into twelve sections, the twelve signs of the zodiac. As the Earth moves around the sun each year, the sun appears to move through each of the twelve signs in turn (astrologers talk of the sun being in Taurus, for example). At the same time, the Earth is spinning about its own axis of rotation, giving us day and night, and this axis is tilted, giving us summer and winter.

As the Earth moves around the Sun, its tilting axis keeps pointing into space in the same direction, or almost so. In fact, the the direction of the Earth's tilt is very gradually changing. This is brought about by the combined attraction of the sun and moon on the bulging equator. The net effect is that the heavens appear to wobble about the Earth, taking approximately 26,000 years to complete a circuit. As a result, our Earth calendar, based on the seasons, slowly moves backward through the zodiac—or, to use the technical term, precesses through the equinoxes—any given date changing signs once every 2,100 years or so.

Astrologers usually take the spring equinox, March 21, as the beginning of the astrological year, and the position of the sun in the zodiac at this equinox determines the characteristic age. (This is the actual position of the sun in the sky, the "sidereal zodiac"; not the "tropical zodiac" that Western astrologers use, which is based on the appearance of the sky several hundred years B.C.) For the last 2,100 years, the sun has been in Pisces at the spring equinox, but it is now shifting into Aquarius. Thus, it is claimed, we are now entering the "Age of Aquarius", an age that astrologers say will be characterized by increasing harmony, high moral idealism, and spiritual growth. Astrologers are divided as to exactly when the transition occurred (or even if it can be given an exact date). But the general consensus seems to be around the late 1960s, with a focusing of votes around 1967.

Whether or not there is anything in such claims is a matter of controversy. Even so, the late sixties, particularly 1967, were certainly a time of transition for many people. It was the heyday of "flower power", and erstwhile hippies still look back with nostalgia to the "Summer of '67". But it was not just a time when people were taking LSD, professing love and peace, and handing out flowers, when facades of houses in Notting Hill, Greenwich Village, and Haight Ashbury were adorned with rainbows and sunbeams. Most of those involved truly believed that if everybody in the world were to have experiences of love and unity, then the world could not fail to be a happier and more peaceful one. A new age could begin; the formula seemed so easy.

The year 1967 itself ended with the Beatles, at the peak of their career, proclaiming "All You Need Is Love". The message was simple—and in many ways, correct. Love *is* all we need. If we could love every other person and every other being, then the world would be many times better, if not ideal. But the question remained: How do you do it? It is no good simply deciding to love, professing love, or act-ing as if out of love. At its best this leads to making a mood of love; at its worst it leads to a rather hypocritical self-contradiction.

What happened to society in the late 1960s is akin to what happens to an individual during the creative process. Creative breakthroughs usually come after a period of pon-dering or incubation, but when they do come they come without any warning, as a sudden flash of insight. The essence of a work of art or the solution to a problem is suddenly clear, the path is obvious. Yet the creative flash then has to be implemented, and it may take months or years of work to put the insight into practice.

The late 1960s probably represented a similar creative flash for society. Suddenly many people saw how the world could be. The flash, however, did not create the reality. The task since then has been to implement this insight, to find ways to raise the consciousness of the individual and bring in love and compassion. In this respect the many New Age movements of the last three decades represent the multitudinous ways in which people are seeking to translate that vision into reality.

New Age or Old?

Not everyone, however, sees the pursuit of self-development in such a positive light. Some argue that such a quest
has little value for the rest of society and generally represents a withdrawal from the real issues facing humanity.
This is the view taken by Daniel Yankelovich, the social
researcher, in his book *New Rules*. He criticizes the search
for self-fulfillment on the grounds that many people's devotion to inner development is antisocial. The emphasis
by Maslow and other humanistic psychologists on the self-
fulfillment ethic is, he argues, "a moral and social absurdity",
giving sanction to desires that do not contribute to society's
well-being. Yankelovich believes that if Western society is
to survive the encroaching crises, we must all make sacri-
fices and begin to pull together; we must be committed to
making society work. Thus, he argues, we must give up
"the inner journey".

Such arguments rest upon a misunderstanding of what
the inner journey is all about. Yankelovich interprets self-
fulfillment as people having everything they want, "a career
and marriage *and* children *and* sexual freedom *and* autonomy
and being liberal *and* having money *and* choosing noncon-
formity *and* insisting on social justice *and* enjoying city life
and country living *and* simplicity *and* graciousness *and* reading *and* good friends, and on and on." If this were the only
type of search for self-fulfillment, he might well be right.

But the pursuits Yankelovich is describing are in many
ways quite different from the self-fulfillment argued for by
Maslow, other humanistic and transpersonal psychologists,
and most spiritual teachers. They are not advocating satis-

fying self-serving needs, the needs of the derived sense of self to find reaffirmation. They are advocating an awakening to one's true Self. This is self-fulfillment in a much more profound sense. Moreover, it is the lack of this much richer type of self-fulfillment that causes people to search for fulfillment in the external world.

Through an inner awakening to the real Self, ego-centered needs can be left behind. This fulfillment of the Self is quite opposite to what Yankelovich believes it to be, and it is this that society needs the most. By tuning in to this deep, unifying level of identity, we may be able to pull together and make society work.

Other people have argued that, even though the goals of the various self-development practices and programs may be laudable and badly needed, many of the people involved appear to be far from enlightened themselves. They sometimes seem egocentric or doctrinaire, as much concerned with their own identity and power as with the enlightenment of others.

Some of those who join a particular group of self-development may be doing so from a sincere desire to unfold more of their potential or discover their inner Self, but others come to keep up with the Joneses, to develop promised mental powers, to be a part of an "in" group, or simply to reinforce their beliefs. People may derive a strong sense of identity from practicing a particular system of meditation, ritual, or life-style, or from being a follower of a particular prophet, guru, or leader. Consequently, the more one affirms one's path to be the best path, the more secure the ego feels. Others become attached to the *idea* of enlightenment, often resulting in the most dangerous ego trip of all, the proclamation that "*I* have transcended my ego", that "*I* am enlightened"—a rather tragic self-contradiction.

Such attitudes and behavior might make us feel more than a little despondent about humanity's chances for true spiritual growth. However, they do not necessarily mean that the practices and techniques themselves lead to ego-dominated activities. We are all subject, to varying degrees, to the need to reaffirm our sense of identity, and even those who have become interested and involved in self-development will still have egos needing some degree of maintenance.

So long as a person still has to realize and integrate the true Self into his life, the means to that goal are inevitably going to be ego-dominated to some degree. Therefore, we should not expect people "on the path" to behave as if they had reached the goal. At least these people are putting their energies in the direction of furthering inner growth rather than hunting whales, strip-mining, building arsenals of nuclear weapons, or pursuing other potentially life-destroying activities.

This gives an intriguing perspective on the evolution of consciousness. For many people, the motivation to discover a higher Self springs from those needs that ultimately will be transcended, the needs of the derived self. In effect, these needs serve as the fuel for their own dissolution. Evolution is, so to speak, pulling itself up by its own bootstraps.

CHAPTER 18

ON THE THRESHOLD

> Everywhere on Earth, at this moment, in the
> new spiritual atmosphere created by the idea
> of evolution, there float, in a state of extreme
> mutual sensitivity, love of God and faith in the
> world: the two essential components of the
> Ultrahuman. These two components are
> everywhere "in the air.". . . Sooner or later
> there will be a chain-reaction.
>
> *Teilhard de Chardin*

Another comment often made about various self-development programs is that they represent a very minor social phenomenon. Some argue that the number of individuals directly involved in inner growth is very small and they are unlikely to have any significant impact on humanity as a whole.

In some respects this criticism is valid; there is little question that the development of consciousness is not at present a widespread human interest. However, if we look at the rapid growth rates on this field, it seems possible that this area of activity could have an extremely significant effect on humanity in the near future.

Earlier we looked at the exponential curve indicative of most natural growth patterns (page 119). We saw that it was characterized by a constant doubling time (the time it takes for the numbers involved to double) which causes the curve to get steeper and steeper. The human mind seems to find it difficult to handle the accelerating nature of the exponential curve (we boggle at world population growth, for example), and when we make predictions about the future of a given growth curve, particularly when we make spontaneous snap predictions, we may not give this acceleration its due. If we are not careful, we may forget that the rate of growth will change and make what is called a linear prediction. Such predictions usually fall far short of the mark.

A good example of such a misjudgment occurred with predictions as to when we could get a man onto the moon. A *Science Digest* article of 1948 declared that, "Landing and moving around the moon offers so many serious problems for human beings that it may take science another 200 years to lick them." A few years later a conference of eminent scientists in England, after lengthy discussion, came to a similar, though slightly less pessimistic conclusion. They declared that we would not see a man on the moon before the year 2000, since it would take that long for all the necessary technological advances to be made. They may have

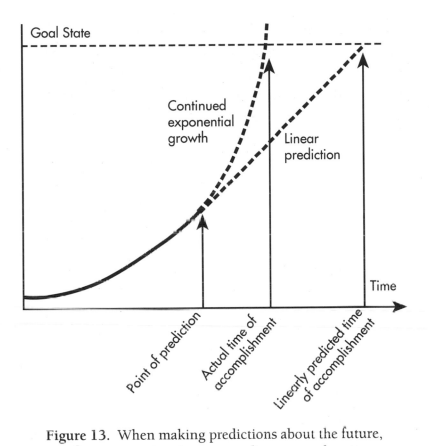

Figure 13. When making predictions about the future, we often unconsciously assume a linear growth pattern. If actual growth is exponential, then a given goal will be reached much sooner.

predicted accurately according to the rate of growth at that time, but what they did not seem to take into account was the rapid acceleration in technological developments that made it possible for a man to be on the moon only fifteen years later.

A more familiar example can be found in the first *Star Trek* series. The TV series was set to happen two hundred years in the future, but within ten years reality had caught up with some of the series' predictions. Captain Kirk refers back to "primitive computers" with magnetic spools. Such computers are already primitive. Kirk's computer also talks with a synthesized human voice, another development that has occurred in one twentieth of the time predicted.

The early *Star Trek* script writers were not being overly naive; very few people in the 1960s were able to foresee the fantastic proliferation of computers and information technology that would take place over the next two decades. What has made its growth so difficult to visualize are the short doubling times involved. The number of people employed in information technology is doubling every six years or so, while computing power itself is doubling every year or so. If today we were to make an on-the-spot prediction of the state of the art in ten years' time, we would most probably base our ideas on current rates of progress and fail to take into account the fact that rates of growth in the future will be much steeper than today. Even our most "fantastic" predictions might fall far short of what is likely to happen.

THE CONSCIOUSNESS CURVE

Rapid as the growth of the information industry is, it may not be the fastest growing area of human activity. There are indications that the movement toward the transformation of consciousness is growing even faster. In terms of sheer numbers the movement may not at present be very significant, but it shows a doubling time of about four years, which makes it one of the steepest growth curves society has ever seen.

Evidence for this comes from several directions. A study I conducted in Britain in 1980 analyzed the rate at which people were becoming actively involved in this field. Five hundred people working on inner growth were interviewed. Although a few of them had been doing so for a long time (some for as many as fifty years), 40 percent had started in this direction within the last four years. An analysis of the overall rate of growth suggested an average doubling time of about five years. Moreover, this growth rate applies to those who had remained involved; those who may have lost interest were not included.

Corroborating data for such a steep rate of growth comes from membership figures supplied by various organizations active in the field of inner transformation. These suggest that many of them are growing with a doubling time of between two and five years. Moreover, the number of such organizations is itself growing rapidly, with what looks like a similar doubling time. If both the number and the size of organizations are doubling at this rate, it would suggest the total number of people involved is doubling even faster. We must take into account, however, the fact that some people may belong to more than one group and thus be counted more than once, and also that many of these organizations may initially go through periods of very rapid expansion, followed by a slowing S-curve of the type discussed in Chapter 7. The net effect of these trends is difficult to compute, but something between three and five years as an overall doubling time seems very likely.

Another way of estimating the growing interest in this

subject is the number of books and magazines published. Analysis of the rate of appearance of new titles in this area suggests they have a doubling time somewhere in the region of three to four years, again, supporting the general trend. All in all, therefore, it seems that if we err on the side of caution and assume a figure of five years for the overall doubling time of interest in this field, we are not going to be far off.

A CONSCIOUSNESS AGE

We started this discussion with the criticism that the various consciousness-raising groups were a minor social phenomenon. But from our analysis of exponential growth, we can see that sheer numbers are not so crucial as the overall rates of growth. These movements are growing faster than the information industries, and if the current trends are sustained, the "consciousness" curve will eventually catch up with and overtake the information curve, however small the former may appear at present.

This trend has been borne out by findings from a series of investigations into changing social values conducted over the last twenty years. Programs such as the *Values and Life Styles Study* in the U.S.A., and the European International Research Institute into Social Change have revealed a steady shift in social values. The number of people motivated by "outer-directed" values, such as the need to feel more materially secure, be approved by others, or be in a position of power, is decreasing; while those motivated by more internal values, such as health and personal development, are steadily increasing.

This rise in "inner-directed" people is manifesting itself in several different ways. It can be seen in the increasing concern with physical fitness, organic food, non-smoking, and other behaviors that contribute to a person's health and well-being. It can be seen in the growing support for aid organizations and environmental groups, as people feel impelled to act on their own sense of right and wrong. It can be seen in the increasing number of people who question currently accepted values and experiment with different, and perhaps more fulfilling, ways of living. And it can be seen in those who are seeking greater inner fulfillment through some spiritual discipline or in other ways of raising consciousness.

Recent studies by Paul Ray at the Stanford Research Institute suggest that these new values are becoming quite significant. In a survey of 100,000 people, sampled to exclude any economic, geographic, or demographic bias, it was found that about 20% of the U.S. population fell into the class of "cultural creatives". These are people with core values of concern for relationships, green politics, idealism, and different ethnic groups. Their numbers were on the increase; whereas other groups, such as "winners" (concerned with status and wealth) and "heartlanders" (concerned with conserving traditional values), were declining. Moreover, this trend is not limited to any one sector of society. It is as evident in executives and homemakers as it is in students and teachers.

Exactly when the consciousness curve will cross the information curve depends upon the percentage of the population currently involved in the movement toward developing consciousness. This is difficult to ascertain at present. Government agencies do not yet consider it to be a phenomenon worthy of analysis. Yet as I write, seven out of ten of the New York Times hardback nonfiction best sellers are "new age/spiritual/consciousness" type books. In terms of general interest the field has already become mainstream.

If it keeps up a doubling time of four years, then it will probably occupy the attention of half the U.S. population—not just the book buying population—by the turn of the millennium. If this sounds astonishing it is because once again our on-the-spot predictions fail to do justice to the rapid acceleration of exponential growth. Remember that only twenty years ago the number of people involved in the computer industry was very small indeed, far smaller than the number now working on expanding individual consciousness; yet look at what has happened to that curve.

Of course, only a proportion of those interested in raising consciousness are actually *employed* in the field (as teachers, therapists, meditation guides, and so forth). But if the growth of general interest continues to swell, so will the number of people employed in this area. We will eventually reach a point, probably sometime early next century, when the employment curve for "consciousness processing" will overtake that of information processing. The evolution of human consciousness would then have become the dominant area of human activity. We would have shifted from the Information Age into the Consciousness Age.

This would represent a time when our needs for food, material goods, and information were being adequately satisfied, and the major thrust of human activity would be able to move on to exploring our inner frontiers. Wisdom

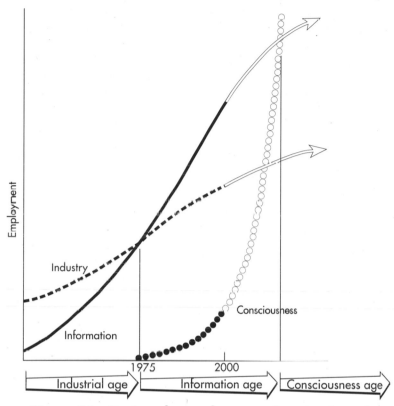

Figure 14. Projected growth curve of proportion of population employed in the field of inner development. If the current rapid rate of growth is sustained, the number of people working in this area could overtake the information curve sometime in the next century.

rather than knowledge would have become our goal. People would be as familiar with practices of self-development and spiritual experiences as today they are familiar with digital watches and compact discs. This may sound like science fiction, but it is a plausible evolutionary speculation, a natural extension of the direction in which some of humanity is already headed.

The above material has been focused on trends within the West, the U.S.A. and Great Britain particularly. They clearly do not apply to the less-developed countries, many of which have not yet even made the transition to the Industrial Age. But as we saw earlier, the lag between the less-developed and the more-developed nations is steadily decreasing, and it should not take as long for the less-developed nations to move into the Information Age as it did for the West. We could likewise expect them to move into the Consciousness Age that much more rapidly, in which case the development of consciousness could well become the dominant human activity over much of the planet within the next century.

In fact, the transition could happen even more quickly than this. First, those who are at present working on inner development are doing so in the context of a predominantly materialistic, externally oriented culture. They are pushing against the inertia of the old consciousness. As the proportion of people reaching higher states of consciousness increases, this inertia will decrease, and at the same time a supportive momentum in the new direction will start building up. The net effect might be that people would begin to find it easier and easier to make progress on the inner path.

The second reason why the transition could come much more rapidly is that we may not have to wait for the majority of a population to be pursuing the transformation of consciousness before we feel the effects. It could be that a small number of people in higher states of consciousness would have a disproportionately positive effect on the rest of society.

Such effects could occur if one person's state of consciousness had, in some way, a direct effect on another's. Strange as this notion might seem, it is not totally implausible; indeed, there is growing evidence that it is happening all the time.

CHAPTER 19

MIND LINKS

In the deeper reality beyond space and time,
we may all be members of one body.

James Jeans

The idea of minds directly affecting each other takes us
into the realm of extrasensory perception, and telepathy in particular. This has long been a hotly debated topic.
The whole field represents a potential crisis for the current
scientific paradigm: experiences such as precognition or
clairvoyance do not fit into the current model of the way
the world works, so either the experience must be explained
away or rejected, or else the model must be changed.

There is not room here to review the current state of
the debate—the briefest survey would fill an entire book—
nor need we be immediately concerned with which effects

are truly "paranormal" (i.e., lie outside normal scientific explanation) and which can be accounted for by orthodox science. The major emphasis of the research to date has focused on specific experiences: Can one person know what another is thinking or feeling? How accurately can he describe images that another person has in his head? Here we will consider less specific effects: the extent to which one person's general state of consciousness and overall brain activity can be directly influenced by those of other people.

This is a relatively new field of investigation, having only received serious scientific attention since mid-1970 (principally because the subject had to await the development of the appropriate research techniques and equipment). One of the early series of experiments in the field was conducted by Russell Targ and Harold Puthoff at the Stanford Research Institute. They took pairs of people who already knew each other well and had a degree of emotional affinity (usually close relatives or couples) and placed them in separate rooms at opposite ends of a building. At randomly selected times, a rapidly flashing light was shone into the eyes of one of the pair. This had the effect of temporarily reducing the overall level of *alpha* activity in the brain. (Alpha activity is a particular electrical brain rhythm usually associated with a relaxed state of consciousness.) Meanwhile, the second person was asked to say when he thought his partner in the other room was experiencing the flashing light. In this task he failed; his scores were no better than those predicted by chance. But although he was not able to "say" what state the other person was in, his own brain showed reduced alpha activity at the same time that the first person's did.

Other researchers have since done similar experiments looking at different physiological variables. Instead of producing a specific brain state in the first person, they put him into a stress situation, measuring the stress reaction by changes in skin resistance and other parameters. Again, the second person could not tell when the first person was under stress, but his skin resistance nevertheless changed. These and similar studies conclude that under certain circumstances, we are in some way receptive to each other's general state of mind, even though on a conscious level we may be unaware of it.

A CONTAGIOUS CONSCIOUSNESS

There is no reason to suppose that such effects are limited to alpha states or states of stress. If the phenomenon is authentic, we should expect it to occur with many other states of consciousness, including the higher states of consciousness associated with enlightenment. And indeed there is considerable testimony to such occurrences in many mystical and spiritual teachings.

An important element of Indian thought is the notion of *darshan*, the belief that an enlightened person can pass on to someone else a taste of enlightenment. Sometimes it may be a touch or a look from the master that confers the experience; sometimes it comes just from being in the presence of an enlightened person. In some traditions the enlightened person need not be there in person, only in mind.

However darshan occurs, the effect is nevertheless considered to be very powerful. The experience is often rather

like that which comes from an exceptionally deep meditation. Sometimes a five-minute encounter can leave one in
a higher state of consciousness for a week. Moreover, this
is not simply a feeling of well-being, one actually experiences aspects of the enlightened state.

It could be argued that such occurrences need not
involve any direct linkage of minds. They may merely show
that, given the right psychological triggers, most of us have
the ability to produce such experiences for ourselves.
Nevertheless, the experience is very powerful and can
radically change a person's life. Somehow or other
enlightenment seems to be contagious.

Similar to this notion is the Christian concept of
grace. Christ is said to have brought to man the grace of
God, and it is through such grace that man can have a
spiritual awakening. The Greek word usually translated
as grace is *charis*. A "charismatic" person originally was
one who bestowed grace, and in the present day there
are many charismatic Christian sects based upon the
belief that a spiritual experience may be directly bestowed
upon a person.

We might hypothesize that comparable transferences
could occur during meditation. Although not in an enlightened state of consciousness, a meditating person will
usually be in a different state of consciousness from the
active person and show different patterns of brain activity.
Another individual close by may begin to show some of the
same changes in brain activity, even though she may be
totally unaware of them. If this second person were also
meditating she might well notice some slight deepening or
facilitation of her own experience. Moreover, her medita-

tion could have a similar effect upon the first person. This mutual feedback process might explain the observation of many meditators that they experience more profound meditations when practicing in a group; the larger the group, the stronger the effect.

GROUP COHERENCE

Such phenomena do not just occur within a room. A study conducted in 1979 has shown they can occur between groups separated by great distances. As part of an ongoing study at Maharishi International University of the effects of collective meditation, a group of approximately three thousand meditators gathered in Amherst, Massachusetts. They were all students of Transcendental Meditation, practicing what is called the "TM-Sidhi Program", an advanced technique that has been found, through a number of studies, to increase the coherence of the brain's activity. (Coherence, in this sense, is a measure of the extent to which different parts of the brain are functioning in step with each other.) The experimenters looked at what effects this group of people, all practicing together, could have on another smaller group practicing similar techniques a thousand miles away in Fairfield, Iowa. Neither the subjects nor the experimenters knew at what times the other three thousand would be sitting to meditate; yet analysis of the brain activity of the second group during meditation showed an increased coherence among individuals whenever the first group was meditating. Coherence between individuals means that the patterns of brain activity in people of the second group were more in tune with each other; their brains became more synchronized.

Just how such effects occur is far from clear, although a variety of theoretical explanations has been put forward. One fascinating theory, which lies within the scope of conventional physics, suggests that during meditation people are setting up resonating electromagnetic waves around the planet, in much the same way as blowing across the top of a bottle can produce resonating waves (a hum). The basis for this hypothesis rests upon the fact that the fundamental resonant frequency for electromagnetic (i.e., radio) waves traveling around the earth (by alternately bouncing off the earth's surface and the upper atmosphere) is 7.5 Hz (7.5 cycles per second). A wave of this frequency, having traveled around the planet, arrives back at its starting point exactly in step with itself, thereby reinforcing itself and setting up a resonance.

It so happens that brain activity during most types of meditation usually includes a strong component at this frequency. Thus, according to this theory, if any faint electromagnetic waves at this frequency were emitted by the brain during meditation, they could set up planetwide resonances; the planet would, so to speak, "hum" with the effects of meditation. The more one resonated with this hum, the deeper the quality of meditation.

The main difficulty with this theory is that any such waves would be exceedingly weak, even with the resonance. Although it has also been found that the brain is particularly receptive to waves of this frequency, it is not at all certain that they would be strong enough to be detected.

There are many other theories that attempt to explain such phenomena. Some are very complex, involving difficult concepts from modern physics, such as quantum field theory; others lie completely beyond the scope of the current scientific paradigm and relate such experiences to a sixth sense or to contact with beings of a higher plane.

Which, if any, such explanations are correct need not concern us here. The important point is that, in some way or other, one person's general state of consciousness appears to set off similar, though generally weaker, effects in other people. This implies that as more and more people in society start experiencing such states of consciousness, other people will gradually pick up the effect, making it easier and easier for them also to reach such states.

MORPHOGENIC FIELDS

Strange as such progress might sound, there are already many instances of such phenomena occurring in nature. In a series of experiments begun at Harvard in 1920 by psychologist William McDougall, rats were being studied to see how quickly they could learn to escape from a maze filled with water. Surprisingly, it was found that successive generations learned the task more rapidly.

Could this be an example of Lamarckian evolution in which parents passed on skills to their offspring? The answer is no. Researchers in Scotland and Australia found that when they came to repeat the experiments, their first generation of rats, bred from a completely separate strain, started at the same level of expertise as McDougall's *last* generation. Some even learned the task immediately without making a single error; somehow they already *knew*. Furthermore, as the experiment progressed, successive generations of the control group, who had never been near the water maze, also improved, along with the experimental group. The skill was somehow learned by other rats, both in the laboratory and across the world.

Rupert Sheldrake, a British plant physiologist, sees this as an example of what he calls "formative causation". In his book, *A New Science of Life,* he proposes that systems are regulated not only by the laws known to physical sciences but also by invisible organizing fields, what he calls "morphogenic fields" (from the Greek *morphe,* form, and *genesis,* coming into being). He sees the regularities of nature to be more like habits than reflections of eternal physical laws. His theory postulates that if one member of a biological species learns a new behavior, the morphogenic field for the species changes, even if very slightly. If the behavior is repeated long enough, its "morphic resonance" builds up and begins to affect the entire species. Thus, in the case of the rats, the more rats that learn the task, the stronger the morphogenic field becomes, and the more easily other rats learn the task.

As another example of formative causation, he cites the difficulty in crystallizing certain organic compounds that have never been crystallized before. Scientists may work for years until they obtain one crystal. But once this has been achieved, other experimenters across the world usually find it much less difficult to produce their own crystals. The more crystals that are produced, the easier it becomes to crystallize the compound.

The conventional explanation has been that microscopic seed crystals are carried from one laboratory to another on the beards or clothing of visiting scientists or by atmospheric currents. But when subsequent crystallizations occur inside sealed containers, as happened with glycerine, this explanation seems to fail. Sheldrake's hypothesis, by contrast, interprets such phenomena as the building up of a particular morphogenic field.

Applying Sheldrake's theory to the development of higher states of consciousness, we might predict that the more individuals begin to raise their own level of consciousness, the stronger the morphogenic field for higher states would become, and the easier it would be for others to move in that direction. Society would gather momentum toward enlightenment. Since the rate of growth would now be dependent on achievements of those who had gone before, we would enter a phase of superexponential growth. Ultimately this would lead to a chain reaction, in which everyone suddenly started making the transition to a higher level of consciousness.

REACHING CRITICAL MASS

Teilhard de Chardin wrote that once sufficient spiritual progress had been made and society had become ripe, then "it would seem that a single ray of such a light falling like a spark, no matter where, on the Noosphere, would be bound to produce an explosion of such violence that it would almost instantaneously set the face of the Earth ablaze and make it entirely new."

Other mystics have suggested that the number of people required to set off such a chain reaction would not need to be that large. For instance, G.I. Gurdjieff, the Russian mystic and teacher, said that just one hundred fully enlightened people would be sufficient to change the world. Alternatively, if enough people were working on spiritual development, significant worldwide effects might still be felt, even though the people had not reached full enlightenment. The Maharishi has claimed that if just one percent of the population were to practice the TM technique, the course of history would be profoundly altered; the "Age of Enlightenment" could dawn.

In order to see how such a small number could possibly have such a profound effect on the rest of society, we might consider a parallel phenomenon in the world of physics, the functioning of a laser. Light, from any source, consists of numerous packets of waves (quanta), each coming from a different atom. In ordinary light these waves are generally out of step with each other; they are said to be "out of phase". If, however, during the brief instant that an atom is about to emit its minute wave packet, light of a specific frequency impinges on it, the atom can be stimulated to emit a light pulse that is in phase with the stimulating wave. As a result, the new emission amplifies the passing wave. At low power the net effect is still one of bundles of waves, out of phase with each other. As the power is increased, a certain level is reached at which a completely new phenomenon occurs. All the little bundles suddenly lock into phase; they are said to become coherent. When they do so, there is a tremendous increase in the intensity of the light produced.

Coherent light increases in intensity because of the different mathematical ways that in-phase and out-of-phase vibrations add up. Waves that are in phase add up as one might expect; a hundred waves acting together are a hundred times as powerful as a single wave. However, waves whose phases are only randomly related will partially cancel each other out; they add up only in proportion to the square root of the total number of waves. A hundred out-of-phase waves, for example, are only ten times as strong as a single wave. Thus a small number of units acting coherently can easily outshine a much greater number acting incoherently. The larger the number of units, the more dramatic the effect. Out of one million units, only one thousand (one tenth of one percent) would need to act coherently for their effect to dominate.

THE MAHARISHI EFFECT

Scientists working at the Maharishi International Univeristy have attempted to apply similar principles to society in an effort to predict how many people will need to rise to higher levels of consciousness before the whole of humanity would be affected. Basing their calculations on the assumption that people who are meditating will not only raise their own levels of consciousness but will have similar effects, however slight, on other people, they have arrived at the figure of one percent as the threshold above which the number of people meditating would have a noticeable effect on a whole city.

That is, of course, only a theoretical model, and a very

simple one at that. Moreover, it is based on rather bold
(and, to some, dubious) assumptions. Nevertheless, most
of the research that has been done on this subject has tended
to support the hypothesis. One indicator of social well-
being that is fairly easy to ascertain is the crime rate. In a
study carried out in 1972, researchers found that crime rates
fell by an average of 8.2 percent in 11 cities in the U.S. in
which 1 percent of the population had learnt TM, but increased by an average of 8.3 percent in 11 matched control
cities. A statistical analysis showed that the probability of
this being a purely fortuitous result was about 1 in 1,000.
More recently, in 1993, 4,000 people gathered for an intensive six-week TM retreat in Washington, D.C. Within three
weeks violent crime throughout the D.C. area had fallen by
18 percent.

To date, more than a hundred similar studies across the
world have revealed similar effects—not only on crime rates,
but also on accident rates, suicide rates, homicide rates,
hospital admissions, and various quality of life indicators.
Such results are truly startling, and one might well wonder
about the quality of the research. Could other factors such
as income, education, unemployment, age, and even the
weather—a well-established influence on crime rates—have
been responsible for the change? Could, for example, an
increased level of education have been responsible both for
the reduction in crime rate and for the growth of interest in
meditation? The general finding was that even when factors such as these were taken into account, meditation
seemed to remain a significant factor.

If a person meditating does have effects such as these
on the rest of society, we might well be headed toward a

threshold point, or critical mass of consciousness, beyond which the momentum of rising consciousness would outweigh the inertia of the old ego-based model. If so, crossing the threshold would represent a major transition for humanity. Beyond it society might be completely transformed.

A CHAIN REACTION

Such sudden transitions are not without evolutionary precedent. At the time of the Big Bang, when the universe was still superhot, any matter that did form would have been annihilated instantly. The surrounding heat (disordered energy) was simply too much for the newly created packet of highly ordered energy. Matter came into permanent being once the temperature had dropped sufficiently (i.e., the general order had increased). Once the conditions were right, however, matter came into being very suddenly. Later, in the primordial soup, life was initially destroyed as fast as it was created. The level of disorder in the surroundings again swamped the highly organized molecular arrangements. Only when a sufficient mass of living systems had been created could life take a permanent hold.

This seems to be a general trend in evolution, and we might expect that at this next step in evolution, the new phenomenon of enlightenment would initially appear and disappear many times, being at first swamped by the prevailing low level of consciousness. Only when the social atmosphere had reached a sufficient level of order and organization (i.e., when higher states were sufficiently widespread) could enlightenment become permanently established.

This is probably the main reason why enlightenment has been such a rare thing in the past: society, as a whole, has simply not been ready for it. In this respect Christ, Buddha, Moses, Mohammed, and all the other great masters were before their time.

The many spiritual teachers who have appeared over the last few thousand years could be compared with the first bubbles of steam that begin to appear in water as it nears its boiling point. At first, it is not hot enough for these early bubbles of steam to be sustained, and they are rapidly reabsorbed back into the water; they are but the heralds of steam. But when the boiling point is reached, there is sufficient energy for them all to fly free, and the water hurriedly turns to steam.

In a similar way, the insights and teachings of the great masters have been distorted and lost once the teachers themselves have died; the wisdom was, so to speak, reabsorbed by the prevailing level of spiritual ignorance. Today, however, the simultaneous convergence of a number of trends could change this. The potential marriage of science and mysticism, the growth of highly efficient methods for disseminating spiritual wisdom, the burgeoning interest in inner development, and the possibility of direct transference of higher states of consciousness are all combining to make it possible, for the first time in human history, for the wisdom of the perennial philosophy to take a firm and lasting hold.

We could be rapidly approaching a time when the "bubbles" of enlightenment would no longer be reabsorbed but would fly free as the whole of humanity begins its great transition. Suddenly everybody would become rishis, roshis, saints, and buddhas. Furthermore, this transition would be occurring at the same time that rapid acceleration in many areas of human endeavor is pointing to a major evolutionary transition and that the connectivity within the human race is reaching a similar complexity to that found in the human brain.

It does indeed seem possible that we alive today could witness the beginnings of the emergence of a high-synergy society, a healthy social superorganism. If so, we could be among the most privileged generations ever to have lived.

CHAPTER 20

TOWARDS A
HIGH-SYNERGY SOCIETY

> The world is now too dangerous for anything
> less than Utopia.
>
> *Buckminster Fuller*

How would the growth of enlightenment in the individual affect society? How would our values change? What would life be like if humanity made the evolutionary leap to a high-synergy society?

One of the first points is that humanity as a whole would be making the transition. The most significant changes, therefore, would occur in the behavior of society rather than of the individual. Consider again the analogy of water coming to the boil. Before the boiling point is reached, the water molecules behave collectively as a liquid. But as the water boils and turns to steam the behavior of the molecules changes radically; they behave collectively as a gas rather than a liquid. The individual molecules, however, have not changed at all, and the laws of quantum physics that apply to each molecule have not changed. It is the relationships between the molecules that have changed. As a result, the laws of steam are very different from those of water. There has been what physicists call "a change of state".

We might expect similar transformations with a major "change of state" in society. The laws of physics, chemistry, and biology would not change dramatically, and each person would continue functioning as an individual biological being: still breathing, eating, drinking, working, playing, making love. The most significant changes would happen at the collective level, as our changed relationships, both with ourselves and with other people, began to give rise to a totally different society. The "laws" of economics, politics, and sociology could change radically, since they are dependent upon collective behavior. They might be as different from current "laws" as the behavior of steam is different from that of water.

Indeed, so different might this new collective behavior be from the way we are today that any predictions we might make could fall far short of the mark. (Could a water molecule that has only known life as a liquid ever guess how things would be after the transformation to steam?) The descriptions that follow, therefore, are of a highly speculative nature—one particular vision of a positive future, a vision of possibilities. As we shall see later, such positive visions are important. Our image of what might lie ahead can play a crucial role in the type of future we create.

A NEW MODE OF CONSCIOUSNESS

To begin with, let us look at some very general features of synergy in society. The essence of high synergy is that the goals of the individual components are in harmony with the goals of the system as a whole. As a result there is minimal conflict between components, as well as between these components and the overall system. Evidence for such decreased conflict in human societies has already been found in studies of some tribal groups that have a naturally high level of synergy; very little aggression was apparent between individuals or between individuals and the group. In a global high-synergy society we might similarly expect a general decrease in conflict and aggression, bringing with it a marked reduction in crime, terrorism, and international hostilities. Once we gained awareness that we are all of the same spirit, all human life would become sacred: war, murder, mugging, rape, and any other form of personal violence would be anathema.

At the very basis of this high-synergy society would be a widespread shift in personal identity. As a result we could expect a reversal of the many inappropriate, wasteful, and often damaging behaviors that stem from the need to reinforce the derived sense of self. Being no longer dependent upon our interaction with the world for our sense of personal identity, we would no longer need to search for positive psychological support and would not be emotionally hurt by negative criticism. There would be no psychological need to gather excess possessions, to belong to the right group, or to adhere to certain beliefs to prove who we are. No longer continually seeking to reaffirm our sense of self, we would be able to act more in accord with the overall needs of a situation rather than with our ego's needs. We would begin to act with true empathy and compassion, born of an immediate experience of oneness.

Furthermore, the widespread development of higher states of consciousness would result in a society where spiritual values were a universally accepted part of life. Self-development and inner growth would be recognized as the proper end of all human striving and the basis of our continued evolution.

Many other long-term goals in this high-synergy society might well be the same as those of contemporary society, for instance, improved health, better nutrition, and more efficient use of energy and mineral resources. From an enlightened state of consciousness, we would feel for the rest of the world much as we now feel for our own bodies, with the result that such goals would not just be intellectually understood as necessary: they would be positively desired and actively realized.

At present, most of us have a spontaneous gut reaction to the idea of deliberately harming our own bodies: chopping off a finger, for example, because it hurts or is in the way. We know, in a very intimate way, that our fingers are part of us. When we have evolved sufficiently so that we feel the same way toward the rest of the world, we would know with an immediate, inescapable awareness that all aspects of the world are as much a part of ourselves as our bodies are. In short, humanity would begin to live in harmony with its environment and with Gaia herself.

Being in tune with each other, humanity, and the rest of the environment would not mean we would all become similar, either in behavior or needs. The cells in your body do not have to become similar in order for you to be a healthy organism; the oneness is at a far deeper level. Likewise, in a high-synergy society, there would be just as rich a diversity of people and interests as there is now. Indeed, freed from the psychological need to belong and conform to a norm, people would be at greater liberty to express their individuality. Rather than everybody tending to become more alike, diversity would increase as a healthy and productive aspect of an evolving organic society.

Similarly, there would be no loss of diversity at the national level; if anything, groups would become more in touch with their particular ethnic and cultural heritages. However, this trend toward increasing diversity would in no way contradict the complementary trend to greater collectivity (e.g., the formation and expansion of transnational groups such as the European Community). Just as in our own bodies the heart, lungs, kidneys, and liver function with a high degree of autonomy and simultaneously work together as part of a larger whole, so in a high-synergy society would there be a synthesis of autonomy and cooperation at all levels from the individual through the family, community, state, and nation and beyond. Social synergy would in no way imply any form of totalitarian world government.

Nor would a shift to high synergy mean that the multitude of problems now facing us would suddenly and magically disappear. The problems of pollution, hunger, energy shortages, mineral shortages, unemployment, poverty, crime, and social, racial, and sexual inequalities would need to be attended to and resolved. This would require individual action, reform movements, and pressure groups; and we would need to put as much, or even more, effort into resolving these issues as we do now.

The crucial difference would be that the very basis of all thinking, analysis, problem solving, and policy making would have changed. The metaparadigm would have shifted. Our world view would be transformed.

No Limits to Growth

One possible consequence of this shift might be a major change in society's attitude toward growth. At present most people see growth in predominantly material terms (with many ensuing problems). With a general shift toward higher states of consciousness, we would begin to see growth in a much wider context; personal and spiritual growth would become as important as, if not more important than, material growth, and our need for material consumption would stabilize naturally.

It is rapidly becoming clear that material growth cannot continue forever; quite soon we are going to start running out of many essential resources. Even before we run out there comes a point where continued growth entails unacceptable social, political, and environmental costs (we may already have reached these operational limits to growth in some areas).

In the late 1980s environmentalists began to talk about

the need for *sustainable development,* and the term was given prominence in Norwegian prime minister Brundtland's report on the environment. More recently, thanks largely to the 1993 Earth Summit in Rio de Janeiro, the term has become common parlance. In essence sustainable development means leaving the planet in as good a state as we found it. Any development we undertake to satisfy our own needs—whether it be an industrial process, a construction project, a new commercial product, or a third-world development project—should not compromise the ability of future generations to satisfy their needs.

However one looks at the notion of sustainable development, one thing is clear: it will require a reduction in consumption. At present rates we will have exhausted our supply of minerals such as copper, lead, mercury, nickel, tin, and zinc within the next fifty years. All the planet's tropical rainforests will have been cut down. And virtually all the petroleum resources will have been consumed within the lifetime of a child born this year.

But few people will willingly reduce their consumption so long as their sense of identity is derived from possessions and material status, or so long as they believe that whether or not they are happy and at peace depends upon what they have or do—an issue that I address more fully in my book *The White Hole in Time.* For when such beliefs dominate our thinking, we come to see our primary needs as material needs, whereas the global crisis is demanding that we move beyond this level of need.

In 1943 the psychologist Abraham Maslow published a now-famous paper in the *Psychological Review,* entitled "A Theory of Human Motivation", in which he identified what

he termed a hierarchy of needs. At the bottom of the hierarchy are the basic physiological needs for food, water, and
oxygen which ensure our day-to-day survival. When these
are satisfied, we turn to the second level, the need for
warmth, safety, shelter, clothing, and long-term survival.
At the third level is the need for love and procreation, en-
suring the survival of the species. Once this has been looked
after, people look for esteem and social status. At the top
of the hierarchy comes the need for self-actualization, the
need to become our true spiritual selves.

Many of us in the developed countries have become
stuck at the fourth level of need, the need for esteem and
status, and we often try to satisfy this by gathering wealth
and material possessions. When we fail to feel fulfilled, we
make the error of thinking that if only we had more or
better possessions, everything would be fine. But since no
material thing can ever truly satisfy our inner hunger, our
material consumption keeps on growing.

If higher states of consciousness were to become the
norm, the root cause of much of our over-consumption
would die away. No longer bound by the needs of the derived self, we would naturally stop consuming products and
services we did not really need. We would realize that, by
and large, we are already able to satisfy most of our material needs and would be free to move on to higher levels of
satisfaction. Society as a whole could then step up the hierarchy to the fifth level of need—self-actualization.

It would seem that the root of the growth problem lies
not in the urge for growth itself, but in our limited awareness of possible avenues of growth. The movement toward
self-realization would allow us to expand our concept of

growth. No longer would we have to curb growth by repressing our material desires, just as when a first-level need such as hunger is satisfied most of us do not have to repress the desire to eat. The field of growth would have risen to a new level, one which brought new and richer possibilities for human fulfillment. Material consumption could then start to decrease without any loss of satisfaction.

Unemployment Revalued

The shift in needs from self-esteem to self-actualization would bring many major changes in values. One change in particular might be our attitude toward work. Traditional areas of employment may very well decrease in the future. Increasing technological innovations and automation in a diverse range of occupations could mean that society would not need everyone to work full time. If, in addition, there were to be a significant shift toward higher states of consciousness, with a consequent decrease in our material needs, employment could drop still further. The net result would be a considerable freeing of time and the opportunity to explore other areas of our lives in greater depth, bringing with it a complete reevaluation of the concepts of employment and unemployment.

Many activities, skills and talents that today are not paid for, because they are not in the short-term interest of any individual, company, or institution, would, in the future, be appreciated for their value to society as a whole. A person might be seen to be benefitting society in the long term in any number of ways not currently regarded as gainful employment: by furthering his own education, passing on his wisdom to others, contributing to the artistic and cultural heritage, or even sitting deep in meditation. As society began to value such activities, the current distinction between salaried employment and unemployment "pay" would need to be reconsidered.

For most people the idea of unemployment still has many negative connotations. These stem from the times in the past when it may well have been necessary for everyone to pull his weight in order that there should be enough food and basic commodities. Although this may no longer be true, it has left us with the attitude that employment is good and unemployment is bad, with the result that the unemployed have often been regarded as second-class citizens. Unemployment, consequently, has become as much a personal crisis as a financial one.

Although some people may perceive a conflict between the right to work and decreasing job opportunities, the real conflict is between the needs for status and financial security and decreasing opportunities to satisfy these needs through employment. In a high-synergy society, the need to reaffirm ourselves through our social status would have died away, and this conflict would diminish markedly. Indeed, it would probably be considered strange to want to work all the time when there would be so much other work to be done on the self.

At present, work is often used as a way of occupying time. This is because our attention is generally outer-directed, feeding on sensory experience. Eight hours of work conveniently fills much of the day; while at home television employs time admirably, as do most other forms of entertainment. Hobbies, housework, social gatherings, conversation, and a few socially acceptable drugs fill in the rest. As a result many people appear to go about their lives on the assumption that they should be left alone with their own self as little as possible.

As needs shift up to Maslow's fifth level, to self-actualization, we could expect to see a growing use of time for inner development. Rather than spending their spare time trying to lose themselves in the world of experience, people would be glad for the opportunity to withdraw from the external world more frequently in order to explore their inner selves. There would be a shift from "the right to work" to "the right to be".

Much of the increased time available might also be spent in education, and not just in the sense of learning and schooling but in its fuller sense of unfolding potential. Education would become a lifelong activity rather than simply a preparation for adulthood.

Currently, most of our intellectual and mental abilities virtually stop growing around the time we finish our formal education, unless we are engaged in activities that require continual updating, reeducation, challenge, and stimulation. With lifelong education the opposite trend would occur: the continued growth and unfolding of our innate, and largely untapped, potentials would become the norm rather than a privilege.

Moreover, the current emphasis of education on facts and information would give way to a balance between the development of knowledge and the development of the knower. Society would enter a new renaissance as creativity, intuition, and personal development became valued as highly as science, technology, and economic development are today. Technological progress would be seen not as a threat to the quality of life, but as a liberator, allowing people to move on in the direction of self-actualization, thereby improving the quality of life in the most fundamental way possible.

Earlier in our history, the division of labor and widespread industrialization freed many people from the need to work on the land, allowing them to spend more time furthering material growth. Today, the increasing application of technology and automation is freeing us from the need to perform tedious manual work, giving us the opportunity to move on to inner growth. In this respect, the reduced need for employment is in line with what seems to be the basic thrust of human evolution: the inner evolution of consciousness.

HEALTHY, HOLY, AND WHOLE

Because the concepts of synergy and health are intimately related, we also ought to expect a high-synergy society to be a healthy one. At present *health* is usually used to mean an absence of any symptoms of disease. Provided your body is functioning reasonably well: temperature, pulse, and blood pressure normal, no recurrent pains, rashes, or fainting spells, you are healthy.

True health, however, means much more than this. The root of the word *health* is the Greek *holos,* meaning whole, and this is also the original meaning of the Anglo-Saxon word *well.* Moreover, the word *holy* comes from the same root. The healthy or well person should therefore be a whole person, one fully developed and integrated in mind, body, and spirit. And the truly whole person would also be a holy person, spiritually mature, that is, enlightened.

In a spiritually transformed society this relationship between synergy and improved health could probably be manifested in a number of ways. First, most techniques that lead to an experience of the pure Self involve physical relaxation and quieting of the mind. One general conclusion of the considerable research conducted on meditation, yoga, and similar techniques is that they produce the exact opposite of the stress response. Blood pressure, heart rate, muscle tension, and other variables commonly associated with stress decrease as do also the levels of various stress hormones in the blood. Stress has also been implicated to some extent in the majority of illnesses, both physical and mental. Therefore, people practicing such techniques should be not only more relaxed but also less prone in general to illness. The few studies that have been conducted in this area tend to support the hypothesis.

Second, in addition to decreasing physiological stress, the thrust toward higher states of consciousness would result in fewer situations being perceived as stressful. This would come, on the one hand, through the decreased conflict and aggression characteristic of high synergy and, on the other hand, from a marked reduction in psychological threats. The vast majority of such threats are only threats to the derived sense of identity. Once the identity has shifted to the pure Self, a major factor in stress would have been eliminated.

Third, there would be fewer man-made health problems. Some of our present ill health is attributable to the exploitive aspects of a low-synergy society: pollution in the atmosphere; toxic wastes finding their way into the drinking water; cancer-inducing additives in foodstuffs and various commercial products; cigarettes, alcohol, sweets, and other known dangers promoted for financial gain. These factors would decrease in a society that lived more in harmony with itself and the world around.

Fourth, we could expect a shift in medical care toward holistic health practices. A common experience of many people engaged in various forms of inner development is that they become more aware not only of their unity with the rest of the world but also of the interplay of mind and body. Through the holistic approach it becomes clear that treating only the physical symptoms (as is frequently the case with Western medicine) and ignoring their psychological and spiritual correlates does not treat the whole system, nor does it ultimately solve the problem.

One effect of this growing awareness would be a greater respect for one's own body. At present some of us exploit our own bodies in our search for ego affirmation: eating the "right" (but often wrong) foods, inviting skin cancer in order to look bronzed, or temporarily escaping reality with a few stiff drinks. With the derived self no longer dominating activity, such behavior would become far less prevalent. We would care for ourselves more. This is the real basis of preventive medicine and the essence of holistic health. It is, in the words of the eco-philosopher Henryk Skolimowski, "taking responsibility for the fragment of the Universe which is closest to one, expressing a reverence toward life through oneself."

In addition, widespread use of holistic health practices would give greater recognition (and responsibility) to the largely unfathomed healing potential of the mind itself. Up until now there has been little mainstream research in this area. What work has been done, however, suggests that we may all have the ability to heal ourselves of anything from a common cold to cancer (we shall be looking a little more into this in Chapter 22). Furthermore, the attitude of mind that seems most to help the ability is very similar to that found in meditation: a state of relaxed attentiveness.

CHAPTER 21

A SYNCHRONISTIC WORLD

Synchroncity is a measure of our inner balance,
our contact with the divine, our wholeness.
Pierre Lutin

Another major consequence of a widespread shift in consciousness could be an increase in those curious and inexplicable chains of coincidences often referred to as synchronicity. Such coincidences might even become the norm, a natural correlate of humanity moving toward a social superorganism.

The celebrated Swiss psychologist Carl Jung described synchronicity as an *acausal*, connecting principle at work in the universe. Acausal events are ones with no apparent physical connection and no way in which they might affect each other. But such events may sometimes be connected in a way that is very meaningful and significant for the people concerned. This is synchronicity, a *meaningful* coincidence. (As such it is different from synchronism, which is merely the simultaneous occurrence of two unrelated events.)

As an example of synchronicity Jung quotes the following case:

> A certain Monsieur Deschamps, when a boy in Orleans, was once given a piece of plum pudding by a Monsieur de Fortgibu. Ten years later he discovered another plum pudding in a Paris restaurant, and asked if he could have a piece. It turned out, however, that the plum pudding was already ordered—by Monsieur de Fortgibu. Many years afterwards Monsieur Deschamps was invited to partake of a plum pudding at a party. While he was eating it, he remarked that the only thing lacking was Monsieur de Fortgibu. At that moment the door opened, and an old man in the last stages of disorientation walked in—Monsieur de Fortgibu, who had got hold of the wrong address and burst in on the party by mistake.

Strange as they might sound, such coincidences are not uncommon. Alan Vaughan, in his book *Incredible Coincidences,* details many such instances. He tells, for example, of a lady who had locked herself out of her house and was busily trying to find another way in when the postman arrived with a letter from her brother returning a spare key he had borrowed. Another typical case is of the person who accidently got off the New York subway at the wrong station, realized his mistake when he reached the exit, and was about to return to the train when he bumped into the very person he was on his way to visit.

BEYOND COINCIDENCE

It could be argued that such coincidences are not statistically significant. We should expect they would happen once in a while. Indeed, for each time a person has a fortuitous meeting, there could be a hundred or a thousand times when no coincidences took place. There is certainly some validity to this argument, and the question that needs to be answered is whether such coincidences occur more often than would be expected by chance alone. Unfortunately, it is practically impossible to gather all the statistics necessary to say whether or not this is the case. Estimating the likelihood of a particular strange coincidence is not that difficult; Vaughan himself carries out such an analysis in several cases and finds the odds sometimes in the order of a trillion to one against. The difficulty lies in assessing the many other unexpected and unlikely coincidences that could have occurred but did not.

There are, however, two general characteristics of such experiences that do suggest they are more than chance and which also have important implications for a high-synergy society.

First, the outcome of such a coincidence generally appears to be beneficial to the person involved, fulfilling his desires or needs at the time. Moreover, one does not benefit from a coincidence at the expense of other people; usually everyone involved finds his own particular needs being fulfilled by the interaction. If these were only chance occurrences, we should expect as many negative as positive outcomes. Yet this does not seem to be the case. Some negative instances have been reported, but they are not so common—and it seems unlikely that people only notice the positive ones. In most cases it appears that the environment is acting in a very supportive manner. Far from being random events, they appear to have a benevolent nature.

Second, the rate of occurrence of such coincidences seems to be directly influenced by the state of mind of the person involved. This is not to say they can be willed to happen. Indeed, deliberate willing could be counterproductive. The man who got off the subway at the wrong station would almost certainly not have done so if he had been consciously trying for such a meeting. Trying is a form of doing, a form of activity in which the individual is manipulating the world. This appears to be the wrong state for such experiences, which seem to occur more frequently when one is in a receptive state, open to some form of unconscious decision-making and flowing with the world rather than pitting oneself against it. Theoretically, then, the occurrence of synchronicity could be encouraged by a relaxed, peaceful state of mind, one which is similar to the state of mind brought on by meditation.

Many people who practice meditation of one kind or another have found that the deeper and clearer their meditations, the more they experience curious patterns of coincidences. This tends to be particularly so after extended meditation retreats; on returning to regular activity, each day can seem like a continual train of the most unlikely, and most supportive, coincidences. Skeptics might argue that people in these circumstances are just more open to noticing synchronicity. But when the coincidences are so remarkable and significant that they influence major aspects of one's life, it is difficult to believe they would otherwise pass unnoticed.

SYNCHRONICITY AND SPIRITUALITY

This relationship between synchronicity and one's state of mind is not a new finding. Twenty-five hundred years ago the Upanishads of ancient India observed that, "When the mind rests steady and pure, then whatever you desire, those desires are fulfilled."

In Christianity we find similar claims. The famous twentieth-century British archbishop William Temple, for example, noted that, "When I pray, coincidences start to happen. When I don't pray, they don't happen." This observation suggests that it may not be the particular supplications in a prayer that are important but the achieving of a state of consciousness that is more open to synchronicity. Indeed, most religious teachings hold that the highest form of prayer is spiritual contemplation, a quieting of the mind and an opening up to the unitive level of consciousness.

We might hypothesize, therefore, that as more people begin to raise their levels of consciousness, synchronicity will become a much more widespread occurrence. Indeed, some people claim this is already beginning to happen. For instance, at Findhorn (a community of several hundred people in the north of Scotland, which focuses on inner growth and loving work) such chains of coincidences are accepted as part of life. Indeed some people feel that we should start to worry when these experiences do not happen, for that is a sign of lack of inner attunement. If higher states of consciousness were to become a reality, perhaps we would have a society in which supportive coincidences were no longer marveled at but accepted as the natural order: a society in which things tended to work out better for everybody.

Returning briefly to the case of a cell in your body, let us consider how it might, if it were aware, likewise experience a form of synchronicity. It might notice that the blood always seems to supply the oxygen and nutrition it needs when it needs them, simultaneously removing waste products as they build up. Such a cell might marvel at the incredible chain of coincidences that keep it alive and provide spontaneous support to most of its desires. Everything would probably seem to work out just right, its prayers continually answered. It might even suppose the existence of some individual answering agency or god.

We, however, looking at the situation from the perspective of the whole organism know that what the cell perceives as a chain of curious coincidences could be ascribed, in fact, to the high synergy that comes from the whole body functioning as a single living being. The cell may not be directly aware of the body as a living system, but it nevertheless benefits from the high synergy that results from this wholeness. Furthermore, the healthier the body is, the more supportive coincidences the cell would notice.

What we regard as curious chains of coincidences might likewise be the manifestation at the level of the individual of a higher organizing principle at the collective level, the as yet rudimentary social organism. As humanity becomes more integrated, functioning more and more as a healthy, high-synergy system, we might expect to see a steady increase in the number of supportive coincidences. A growing experience of synchronicity throughout the population could, therefore, be the first major indication of the emergence of a global level of organization.

ESP and the Miraculous

Related to synchronicity are paranormal phenomena such as telepathy, clairvoyance, and precognition: what are collectively known as extrasensory perception, or ESP. Despite numerous attempts to find a cause-effect explanation for such phenomena, no one has yet explained satisfactorily how they might occur. To some this might seem sufficient reason to reject their validity. But others, such as Jung, have seen them to be examples of synchronicity phenomena, an indication of a higher organizing principle beyond the causal space-time arena within which most science deals. If we accept this view, then it seems likely that a general increase in synchronicity could also lead to an increase in ESP.

To some people ESP suggests the idea of being able to "read another person's mind", or "predict the winner of a horse race". While such things may be possible, this is not the way such phenomena usually manifest themselves. Telepathy, for example, means literally "feeling at a distance" (*telepathos*), and these experiences do indeed seem to happen more often on the feeling level. One is more likely to have a *feeling* that a close friend is ill rather than a sudden clear message from the friend.

It might be thought that such abilities, if they do exist, are the attributes of very few. But recent research suggests that we may all have these faculties latent within us. Targ and Puthoff, who conducted some of the research into the alignment of EEG patterns mentioned earlier, also carried out a series of pioneering experiments in what has become known as remote viewing. In a typical experiment involving two people, the *receiver* would remain in the laboratory, while the *sender* would visit a randomly chosen location, unknown to the receiver or the experimenters. He or she would then spend some time looking around and taking in the environment as fully as possible. During this time the receiver in the laboratory would draw or describe any images that happened to come to mind. Later these drawings and descriptions were matched by an independent panel with the various possible locations the sender could have visited. The match turned out to be much greater than would be expected by chance alone.

Targ and Puthoff began their experiments with people who already seemed to have well-developed psychic abilities but later found that anyone could be equally successful in describing that target location. The office secretary, for example, who claimed no special abilities, scored as well as the acknowledged psychic. What seemed to be important was a general willingness and openness to explore in greater depth some of the faintest images and hunches that often pop up in the mind which we ordinarily might reject as spurious or irrelevant. Studies such as these suggest that ESP almost certainly occurs much more widely and frequently than we are aware of.

Other experimental work suggests that it may be the more visual right side of the brain, rather than the verbal-analytical left, which is involved in these phenomena. Perhaps our tendency to concentrate more on the skills associated with the left hemisphere—language, logic, and linear thinking—has resulted in many of us not experiencing telepathy and other forms of ESP. People seem to be much more accurate in ESP experiments when asked to describe the *images* they have, rather than their verbal ideas. (It has been observed that people with left-brain damage are often better in ESP tasks, probably because there is then less interference with the right-brain functions.) A receptive state of mind, which is considered to be a characteristic of the right brain, also appears to be conducive to ESP. As with other forms of synchronicity, it is very difficult to *make* these things happen.

If, therefore, higher states of consciousness do lead to an integration of the left and right sides of the brain, we might also expect them to lead to a more widespread occurrence of ESP. This contention is supported by many spiritual teachings that suggest these abilities develop quite naturally as one's level of consciousness rises.

SUPERNORMAL POWERS

ESP is not, however, the only paranormal faculty likely to develop in a society of the spiritually enlightened. The writings of most spiritual traditions and many mystics suggest that various other abilities would emerge, some of which might make ESP seem like spiritual kindergarten.

Indian traditions, for example, speak of powers called *siddhis* which come as a result of enlightenment. The *Yoga Sutras,* an ancient text that is the cornerstone of yogic philosophy, describes some fifty-two powers, ranging from telepathy and clairvoyance to invisibility, levitation, walking on water, and being in two places at once.

The *Anguttara Nikaya,* a collection of the Buddha's teachings, describes similar supernormal abilities: "There is the one who. . . having been one becomes many . . . appears and vanishes, unhindered he goes through walls. . . . He dives in and out of the earth as if it were water. Without sinking he walks in water as if on earth. Seated cross-legged he travels through the sky like a winged bird." Not only was the Buddha himself said to be endowed with such powers, but so were hundreds of his monks.

Reports of these abilities have not been confined to the East. In Christian scriptures we find Noah, Elijah, Isaiah, and Christ displaying similar powers. In Christ's case this is sometimes seen as proof of his divinity, yet he himself claimed that such capacities were open to anyone: "You shall be able to do all these things and more." Peter, once he had seen Christ walk on water, was able to do it himself—until he "lost faith".

Many other holy people and saints are said to have performed similar miracles: St. Theresa of Avila and St. John of the Cross, two medieval Christian saints, were witnessed by many to have levitated. And Catherine of Sienna and Joseph of Copertino were credited with similar abilities. Indeed, so much are such powers seen to be a natural outcome of spiritual development, the Roman Catholic Church has made the performance of miracles a prerequisite for official canonization.

Physical science remains unable to explain how such phenomena could possibly take place; in most cases they directly contradict the current paradigm. Many would therefore reject any such claims as "impossible", relegating them to an overzealous account of quite ordinary events or even to pure fantasy. Yet the fact that so many teachings from around the world repeatedly affirm their occurrence suggests that we ought not to dismiss them completely, even though we may not yet understand them or have experienced them ourselves.

If it turns out that such claims are valid, we might well find that a society of enlightened people would be a society in which we all had these faculties. Unbelievable? Too far-fetched? Such phenomena might be an indication of just how profound the transformation could be—a water molecule's glimpse of steam.

Whether or not such abilities would be a part of a spiritually transformed society, and whatever additional unforeseen developments might occur, we are still left with the question: Could a high-synergy society really happen?

Granted, there seem to be a number of indications that humanity is heading toward a major evolutionary leap, and that such a transition, if it were to occur, might not be centuries away. But it certainly is not inevitable. The choice of whether or not we do move in this direction rests very much with us.

CHAPTER 22

CHOOSING THE FUTURE

Shortage of time is the greatest shortage of our time.
Fred Polak

Throughout this book I have deliberately taken a very optimistic view of humanity and its future. Why? More than because optimism is enjoyable, and more than because I very much hope for this kind of future. I have taken a positive perspective because I believe that the image we hold of the future plays a role in helping that future to emerge. If I entertained a negative scenario and encouraged others to hold that view, I would be instilling a negative mental set about the future and would be helping to make a negative future more likely. By the same token, encouraging positive visions of the future may actually help us move in a more positive direction.

Our dominant image of the future today is generally a pessimistic and depressing one. The majority of people take it for granted that the chances of some form of collective calamity are high. Moreover, most of the information we receive about the world supports this negative image. Newspapers and news bulletins effectively chronicle the problems and disasters of the day. News, it seems, means bad news.

As society becomes increasingly despondent about its own future, it seems to produce more stories of doom to reinforce its gloomy mind set. For example, a recent survey of the films being shown in London (excluding pornographic films) revealed that over 80 percent involved disaster, disruption, or violence of one form or another. This kind of media exposure tends to reinforce the image of society moving in the direction of collapse. Negativity seems to breed negativity.

Indian teachings have summed this up in the saying *"Sarvam-annam"* (All is food). By *all* is meant not only the food we eat and the air we breathe but what we take in through the senses as well. Negative, destructive, or aggressive perceptions can have a negative, destructive, or aggressive effect on our consciousness. In effect it is possible to pollute our minds just as we can pollute the physical world around us, and this mental pollution can affect our lives as radically as physical pollution, if not more so.

A study in Great Britain, reported in the *New Scientist,* showed that the violence of news reports led to a more violent attitude in children who viewed them. Those who watched the local Northern Irish news bulletin, which contained about four times as many references to violence as the BBC national news, developed a considerably more violent attitude than those who watched the national news, irrespective of whether they lived in Northern Ireland or mainland Britain.

Yet, contrary to what many news editors apparently believe, a study in the U.S.A., published in *New Age Journal,* found that when negative news bulletins were replaced by positive ones, people found the news just as enjoyable. More significantly, they began to change their attitude toward the people they met in daily life, seeing them in a much more positive light.

But the mindsets we have of society appear to have an impact that goes far beyond individual attitudes and behavior. In his book *The Image of the Future,* Fred Polak, a Dutch futurist, showed that our images of the world play a crucial role in shaping society. He found that in every instance of a flowering culture there had been a positive image of the future at work. As an example, he noted the way in which the Jewish people have remained spiritually intact over centuries of adversity. Israel's power, he suggested, rested in her living image of the future; the power of the prophets and the revolutionaries came from a burning expectation for the future. When the opposite occurred, when images of the future were weak, the culture decayed as in the case of the fall of the Roman Empire.

Polak also found that the potential strength of a society was reflected in the intensity and energy of its images of the future. These images acted as a barometer, indicating the potential rise or fall of a culture. This intimate relationship between the image of the future and the future itself could make it possible to predict the direction cul-

tures would take. He concluded that "bold visionary thinking is in itself the prerequisite for effective social change."

IMAGES THAT HEAL

Images that are held in the mind can also have a profound
impact on human physiology and may play a crucial role in
healing. Much recent work in this area has centered on the
role of mental images in the treatment of cancer, and this
research will be worth considering briefly, since it offers
clues as to another possible approach for healing the planetary cancer.

Western society's general attitude toward cancer is a
negative one: it is seen as a potentially fatal illness, widespread and difficult to cure. So negative are our sets that in
some areas of society it is taboo to mention the subject or
to admit that one personally has some form of cancer. For
the patient this negative image is compounded by prog-
noses about his chances for survival. If he is given the
mental set that he has six months left to live, and this is
backed up with the authority of doctors, he usually fulfills
the predictions—a fact that aboriginal witch doctors know
only too well.

At the same time, however, there have been many well-
established instances of spontaneous remission, in which
the cancer patient gets better of his own accord in spite of a
negative prognosis. In a number of these often dramatic
recoveries it was found that for one reason or another—
perhaps as the result of a deep, spiritual experience, or falling
in love—the person changed his whole attitude toward life

and regained a strong will to live. Generally speaking, the more positive the outlook, the greater the chances of remission.

This healing power of the mind is being studied by several cancer specialists, who are finding that many malignancies seem to respond positively to the use of imagery. Two pioneers in this field were Carl and Stephanie Simonton, working in Dallas, Texas. They found that if a patient is taken into a state of deep relaxation and in this state visualizes his white blood cells swarming over the cancer cells, consuming them and carrying them away, then very often the malignancy ceases growing and starts shrinking. In many cases it has disappeared completely.

They also noticed that the more hopeful or powerful the imagery, the better the result. If, for example, a patient visualized the cancer as a large logjam blocking a river, being attacked by just one man—a single white blood cell—then the imagery conveyed little hope of success and was not very effective. But, if the white blood cells were seen as a vast army of knights on horseback charging through the landscape killing the much smaller, slow-moving cancer cells, the imagery had a much more powerful effect. Optimism, it appeared, was crucial.

In many respects humanity itself is behaving rather like a malignant growth on the planet, and it was suggested earlier that both the general behavior and the root causes of humanity's malignant tendencies bear close similarities to cancer in the body. Perhaps, then, some of the principles being applied in the Simontons' work can also be applied to helping heal the planetary cancer.

There appear to be two key elements in their approach:

The subject has, first, a relaxed, almost meditative, state of mind, and, second, a specific image of the desired result. One of the effects of relaxation is to increase the synchrony of the brain activity; that is, the firing of the cells becomes more in step. What would produce a corresponding synchrony in the global nervous system? As was seen earlier, this might be a result of people meditating together, coming into tune through the universal Self.

What then might be the effect of a million people across the world, meditating simultaneously, and from the depth of their meditation visualizing, for example, the whales of the world no longer being pursued and killed, but growing in numbers and cared for by humanity; or maybe visualizing the long-term peaceful settlement of some international dispute, seeing the parties concerned agreeing on a mutually satisfactory solution? Might we see a collective synchrony? Might there come an end to whaling or the settlement of the dispute?

Of course, the answer is not at present clear. Some who have tried such collective imagery do claim positive results, but in light of the shortage of well-controlled studies, skeptics could claim justifiably that such results might only be coincidental.

One could argue, however, that at the present time only marginally significant results could be expected. First, there is still the collective inertia of the "old consciousness" to be battled. Second, the experiments so far have not generally involved very large numbers of people, nor have the images always been that specific. And third, the techniques of meditation employed may not always have produced sufficient access to the more universal levels of consciousness.

Thinking of a tumor dissolving is not as powerful as sitting in a particularly quiet state with specific images of white blood cells battling and eliminating the malignant cells. Similarly, getting people simply to sit down at a certain time and to imagine a world peace—valuable though this may be—is not likely to be as beneficial as using specific techniques to produce the right state of consciousness, and then using very specific mental images of the desired results. As psychotechnology becomes an established and productive area of scientific research, we may discover just what state of consciousness and imagery are best for this sort of endeavor and how to most effectively and efficiently induce them.

This suggestion may sound "way out" to some, and only time will tell if it is possible. However, if such approaches are found to produce significant effects, they could become a very powerful adjunct to meditation in furthering planetary healing. Indeed, they could be one of the most powerful agents for change that humanity has had at its disposal.

Our Evolutionary Exam

To hold a positive image of the future does not mean that we should fill our minds with naive optimism and sit back hoping that all will be well. Humanity is indeed in a state of severe crisis, and there is no law of nature that says we will necessarily survive. Even if humanity does experience the kind of transformation envisioned here, the current problems are almost certainly going to get steadily worse, and we may have to descend into some very major global instabilities before a new level of integration finally emerges.

From the perspective of dissipative systems theory, these crises can be seen as the catalysts pushing humanity on to a new evolutionary level. If humanity successfully adapts to the crises, it could break through to a higher level of organization. But if it fails to adapt, because the crises prove to be too severe, then society may break down and collapse completely.

There are indeed any number of collective disasters that could befall us before the general level of consciousness has risen sufficiently to bring about the needed transformation. Even if we do manage to avoid these awesome catastrophes, many other negative scenarios are still possible: increasing terrorism, crime, and personal violence; nations fighting each other as they greedily grab what they can of dwindling resources (a fight that has already begun); economic collapse bringing roving hoards out of the cities in search of food; ghettoes spreading across continents. Alternatively, it is possible that we may manage to continue on our present path, dealing with today's problems in the same partially successful ways we have tried so far. Humanity might not collapse, but neither would it move on to become an integrated social superorganism.

If we do not make the transition, it might be thousands of years before humanity stands on the threshold again. Or it might never happen with the human species. If we wipe ourselves out, it could take millions of years for another species to evolve with the same potential. Or the transformation might never happen on this planet at all. But there are plenty of other planets in our galaxy, and plenty of other galaxies. The universe will carry on evolving toward higher levels of integration and complexity whether we do or not.

If, however, humanity does find ways to resolve the various problems and conflicts facing it, it will have proved it can adapt successfully. In this respect crises not only serve as evolutionary catalysts but also as evolutionary tests, examining the adaptability and viability of the system. Indeed, humanity's currently growing set of crises could be seen in this light: We may have reached our final test of our viability for further evolution

A Cosmic Intelligence Test

This test, of course, is not a physical test. It is a test of our true intelligence. It is an assessment of whether or not humanity is psychologically and spiritually fit to live on planet Earth, whether we can change at a very fundamental level the way we relate to others and the environment, whether we can work in harmony rather than conflict, whether we can balance centuries of material progress with an equal amount of inner growth, whether we can connect with that level of unity that we know theoretically (and, in those privileged, magical moments, know experientially) lies at our core.

Moreover, this test has a time limit. We do not have eons to experiment. We who are alive today need to respond to these questions.

Whether or not we pass is up to us. If we do pass, we may move into our next evolutionary phase, our integration into a single being. If we fail, we will probably be discarded as an evolutionary blind alley, an experiment that for one reason or another did not quite work out. Humanity will be spontaneously aborted, regardless of how close to the transition we might seem to be. If so, we will not be the first species to have become extinct on account of its failure to adapt.

Mother Nature, from her cosmic perspective, is not going to be too perturbed if we do not make it. She is not brought to despair by every blade of grass that is crushed underfoot, by every cell that dies, or by every seed that fails to germinate. Indeed, if humanity is aborted it will be for good reason. As far as Gaia as a whole is concerned, it might be as satisfactory an outcome as if we had passed the test.

But the task of showing whether or not humanity is viable rests with us—each of us. Unlike other species, humanity can anticipate the future, make conscious choices, and deliberately change its own destiny. For the first time in the whole history of evolution, responsibility for the continued unfolding of evolution has been placed upon the evolutionary material itself. We are no longer passive witnesses to the process but can actively shape the future. Whether we like it or not, we are now the custodians of the evolutionary process on Earth. Within our own hands—or rather, within our own minds—lies the evolutionary future of this planet. We can *choose* to carry ourselves through.

Will we be able to choose in time?

No one can say. But as long as the door is open to us and as long as the evolutionary impulse shines through us, let us follow that inner urge. This is the cosmic imperative.

EPILOGUE

CHAPTER 23

BEYOND GAIA

> A walker in mountainous country, lost in mist, and groping from rock to rock, may come suddenly out of the cloud to find himself on the very brink of a precipice. Below he sees valleys and hills, plains, rivers, and intricate cities, the sea with all its islands, and overhead the sun. So, I, in my supreme moment of my cosmical experience, emerged from the mist of my finitude to be confronted by cosmos upon cosmos, and by the light itself that not only illuminates but gives life to all.
>
> *Star Maker, Olaf Stapledon*

If humanity were to evolve into a healthy, integrated, social superorganism, this transformation could signal the maturation and awakening of the global nervous system. Gaia might then achieve her own equivalent of self-reflective consciousness, and a new level of evolution, the Gaiafield, might emerge. Gaia would become a conscious, thinking, perceiving being, a being functioning at a new evolutionary level with faculties quite literally beyond our imagination.

What would she discover if she were to awaken?

First, she would become aware of her immediate environment, our solar system. She would begin to study the space around, the nourishing sun, the other planets and their moons, looking to see if there were any signs of life out there. Indeed, this she has already begun.

Over the last two decades, Gaia's nervous system has begun to sense the space around. Ten thousand artificial satellites have been put into orbit; probes have taken a closer look at all the planets. Others have visited asteroids, comets, the sun, and some have even gone beyond the solar system, sending back information about the outer space beyond. Seen from a distance, it would look as if Earth were beginning to grow nerves out into the solar system, fine tendrils sensing her immediate environment.

Already she has discovered that this solar system contains far more than the sun and its nine known planets. There are at least thirty-eight natural moons circling the planets and thousands of asteroids in between the planets. There are also several million comets in orbit around the sun, some of which have orbits so huge they effectively extend the solar system halfway to the next star.

In addition to the many comets, moons, and asteroids, there is the solar wind, a stream of charged particles emitted by the sun, which flows far into the reaches of outer space. Also flowing out deep into space are the VHF radio and TV signals created by humanity over the last fifty years.

Traveling at the speed of light, Gaia's emissions have already swept past the thousand or so stars nearest to us.

If we could perceive the orbits of the comets, the solar wind, and the ever-expanding waves of radio signals, we would see our solar system, not as an isolated group of objects moving round the sun, but as a huge complex sphere of influence penetrating deep into the heart of other solar systems.

FROM GAIA TO GALAXY

Gaia's explorations so far indicate there is little life elsewhere in this solar system, certainly not rich biosystems from which other Gaias might emerge. But what of other solar systems? As Gaia continues her explorations and looks beyond this solar system, will she find other conscious planetary beings out there also seeking contact? The answer could very well be yes.

Our solar system is minute compared to the whole galaxy. If we imagine the North American continent to represent our galaxy, then the Earth would be a mere ten-thousandth of an inch, and its orbit the size of a pinhead; the sun would be the minutest speck visible to the naked eye in the center of this pinhead; and the volume occupied by the whole solar system would be about the size of an apple, an apple hidden somewhere in North America.

According to current estimates, there are some hundred billion (10^{11}) stars in our galaxy, a good percentage of which probably have planets accompanying them. Astronomical observations of the seventeen stars nearest to the sun have

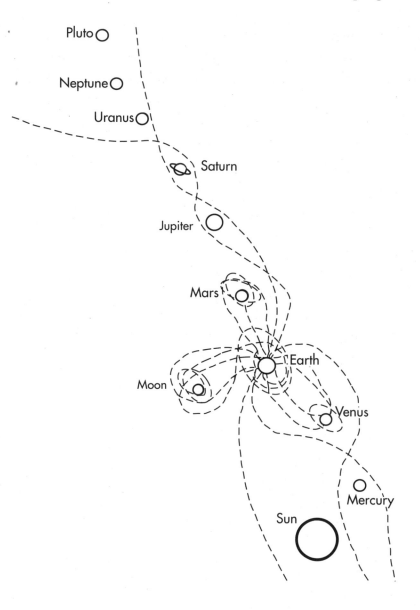

Figure 15. Gaia's growing nervous system, sensing her immediate environment through humanity's exploration of space. (Not to scale.)

found that at least four show signs of having planetary accompaniments. Furthermore, computer simulations of star formation suggest that the cloud of gas that surrounds a newborn star is very likely to condense into a planetary system, and that the systems that result would usually be reasonably similar to our own solar system in their general structure—rocky, Earth-like planets near the star and larger, colder, Jupiter-like planets farther away. Of these solar systems, it is estimated that in our galaxy alone there may be as many as 10^{10} with planets capable of supporting life as we know it.

How many of these planets would actually develop life? Maybe most of them. As far as the Earth is concerned, once the conditions for the emergence of life were right, life appears to have dawned very rapidly; it seems to have been a virtual inevitability. Furthermore, the Gaian tendency to preserve the optimal conditions for the maintenance and further evolution of life suggests that, once it had gained a foothold, life was unlikely to die out. If these are general tendencies to be found throughout the universe, we should expect life to emerge and evolve on virtually every viable planet, protected and nurtured by the planet's own respective Gaia. Thus the number of potential Gaias within our galaxy could well be of the order of ten billion.

As we explored earlier, ten billion seems to be the approximate number of units required in a system before a new level of evolution can emerge. Could the possibility of ten billion living planets in our galaxy herald the emergence of some galactic superorganism whose cells are awakened Gaias?

Applying the same criteria as we used for the emergence of a social superorganism, we can see that ten billion Gaias distributed through a galaxy would not, on their own, create a galactic superorganism. There would also need to be a widespread communication and connectivity between the many Gaias, similar to the degree of complex interaction and organization found in the human brain.

How might these Gaias communicate and interact? Interplanetary expeditions would be far too slow; a single voyage across the galaxy would take millions of years. Electromagnetic communication, whether by light, radio, infrared rays, or X-rays, would be much faster. Yet even at the speed of light it would take thousands of years for a message to cross the galaxy. Although this may only be a minute in the life of Gaia, it is probably still too slow for a highly complex web of communication to emerge. Perhaps the various forms of ESP are not limited by the speed of light; if so, they could enable much faster and more complex connections to develop. In addition, there could be means of interaction characteristic of the Gaiafield itself that we cannot conceive, and these could serve to enhance inter-Gaian contact.

If, one way or another, Gaias were able to reach out, make contact, and interact with each other, there could then come a time, millions of years from now, when inter-Gaian interaction and communication would reach a sufficient degree of complexity and synergy for the ten billion Gaias in this galaxy to integrate into a single system. Our own solar system might no longer exist then; stars in the galaxy come and go as do the cells in a living organism. Even if our Gaia were still alive, humanity might have evolved be-

yond recognition, or perhaps new life-forms would have
arisen, taking over humanity's role.

Regardless of when this might occur, this next evolutionary step would signify the transition to a galactic
superorganism. The galaxy would become its equivalent
of conscious. With this might come the emergence of a
sixth level of evolution, one as different from the Gaiafield
as the Gaiafield is from consciousness, consciousness from
life, and life from matter.

FULL CIRCLE

We likened the size of our own solar system in the galaxy
to an apple in North America. Yet this galaxy is but itself a
minute structure in the whole universe, another apple lost
on another huge continent. So huge are the dimensions
involved that it is almost impossible to conceive of just how
big the universe is, and just what a minute speck in it our
own galaxy is.

On a clear night we may look up at thousands of stars
filling the sky, yet with only one or two exceptions, every
point of light we see, however faint, is a star within our
own galaxy. We are seeing less than a billionth of the universe. When we look into space through a powerful
telescope, we find that the dark patches between those stars
are filled with myriads of tiny points of light. Moreover,
each of these specks is not a star but a whole galaxy. And
these are just the galaxies close enough to be seen.

Looking at the distribution of these galaxies, astronomers have found that they are not scattered randomly

throughout space; they tend to group together in clusters. Some clusters are small, containing ten or twenty galaxies, while others may contain as many as a thousand galaxies.

Our own galaxy is part of a small cluster containing twenty-seven known members, and all around our local cluster are similar clusters of galaxies. In the middle of these is a very much larger cluster, called the Virgo cluster, containing thousands of galaxies. Seen from far out in space, our local cluster appears to be part of a huge cloud of clusters, all centered on the Virgo cluster. This entire system is called the Virgo Supercluster. Looking out even farther into space, astronomers find the universe filled with numerous other similar superclusters, each containing thousands upon thousands of galaxies.

If we liken an entire galaxy to a single atom, then what astronomers are observing is reminiscent of the way in which atoms collect to form simple molecules, which in turn group to form macromolecules. If thousands of macromolecules can build up a living cell, then perhaps the numerous superclusters themselves could gather into a single system? Could the universe as a whole become a single living system?

When, at the start of our journey, we looked at the possibility of our planet being a living system, we found a number of strange coincidences that happened to provide the optimal conditions for the evolution of life. They were either a very unlikely and very fortunate series of flukes or the planet was somehow purposefully maintaining this optimum. Physicists are now discovering that some similar strange coincidences appear in the universe as a whole.

For some unknown reason, slightly more electrons than

positrons (antielectrons) were created in the Big Bang. Since electrons and positrons annihilate each other when they meet, when this canceling out was complete, some electrons remained. These remaining electrons became the basis of all the matter now in the universe. Were the initial numbers of electrons and positrons equal, we would have no galaxies, no stars, no planets, or even any gases.

If the early universe had expanded at a slightly different rate, it would have ended up very differently: a fraction slower and it would have rapidly collapsed in upon itself to form a black hole; a fraction faster and galaxies would never have had the chance to condense.

If the fine structure constant of nuclear physics were different by a very small amount, the rate at which hydrogen converts into helium would be significantly changed. If the rate were a little slower, the universe would have remained predominantly hydrogen; slightly faster and it would have become predominantly helium. Either way, stars as we know them would not have evolved.

If the ratio of the masses of the electron and proton were as little as 1 percent different it would have been impossible for complex molecules to form.

If the nuclear forces that bind atomic particles together had varied in strength by more than 2 percent, no heavy elements would have been formed. There would have been no basis for life.

If the gravitational force had been a fraction larger, there would have been no convection within stars, no thermal instabilities leading to supernova explosions, no heavy elements scattered into space, and no evolution of matter toward more and more complex forms.

If just one of these factors had varied, the universe as we know it would not exist. Could this all be the result of a tremendous series of flukes? Or rather is it possible that the whole universe, like Gaia, is somehow organized so that living systems can evolve? If so, could the universe as a whole be headed toward becoming a single universal being?

If, over thousands of millions of years, the ten billion galaxies in the universe not only evolved into galactic superorganisms but also began to interact and communicate with each other, then there might come the final stage of evolution: a universal superorganism. A seventh level of evolution might then emerge, a level we could call "Brahman", after the Indian word for the wholeness of the universe in both its manifest and unmanifest forms.

If this were to be the final evolutionary development, it would in some respects bring the whole process full circle. Beginning from a unity of pure energy, the universe would have evolved through matter, life consciousness, Gaias, and galaxies to a final reunion in Brahman. From a unity of total nondifferentiation it would have evolved, through the most multifarious diversities, to a unity of total integration. From Brahman to Brahman.

What then?

The universe could possibly collapse in upon itself in some kind of "Big Wumph". Would that be the end? Or would it just be the end of one cycle of the universe?

Maybe another Big Bang and another long chain of evolution would follow? Perhaps in the next universe there would be a very slight change in the physical constants so that the universe could evolve a little differently. Each cycle might be a fresh experiment, a slight improvement on the previous one—an evolving of evolution itself. If so, Brahman would, so to speak, be reincarnated in each fresh cycle, each time becoming a more perfect universal being. And the ultimate goal of the universe might be the enlightenment of Brahman: the perfect cosmos.

In that final union could come the time of which Olaf Stapledon dreamed in his book *Star Maker*:

> This final creature. . . embraced within its own organic texture the essences of all its predecessors; and far more besides. It was like the last movement of a symphony, which may embrace, by the significance of its themes, the essence of the earlier movements; and far more besides. . . .

> And the Star Maker, that dark power and lucid intelligence, found in the concrete loveliness of this creature the fulfillment of desire. And in the mutual joy of the Star Maker and the ultimate cosmos was conceived, most strangely, the absolute spirit itself, in which all times are present and all being is comprised.

FURTHER READING

The following list includes books mentioned in the text, books that complement the themes developed here, and books that have inspired me. Each of them is highly recommended for further reading.

BARROW, JOHN D. and FRANK J. TIPLER. *The Anthropic Cosmological Principle.* Oxford: Clarendon Press, 1986. If you do not like books that are full of mathematical equations, then this is not for you. But if you do, this is the most thorough work so far on the hypothesis that the universe may, after all, have a design to it.

BENTOV, ITZHAK. *Stalking the Wild Pendulum.* New York: Dutton, 1977. A creative and holistic view of human consciousness and the universe, drawing on holography, quantum physics, and Transcendental Meditation. Fun and mind-opening.

BOULDING, KENNETH. *The Meaning of the Twentieth Century.* New York: Harper and Row, 1965. An economist's visionary analysis of "the great transition", the transition to a postindustrial society, and its evolutionary significance.

Brown, Mark. *The Dinosaur Strain.* Shaftesbury, England: Element, 1988. The best introduction to mindsets, how they affect us, and how they can be used constructively. Entertaining and thought-provoking.

Capra, Fritjof. *The Turning Point.* New York: Simon and Schuster, 1982. A thorough and grounded examination of how the present crises in economic, social, political, medical, educational, and other spheres are reflections of an outdated world view. Written concurrently with the first edition of this book, Capra's book looks more closely at many of the issues I have raised. Highly recommended.

Curle, Adam. *Mystics and Militants.* London: Tavistock Publications, 1972. A balanced and thorough look at the old debate between militant action and inner growth, with a penetrating analysis of the role of belongingness-identity.

Ferguson, Marilyn. *The Aquarian Conspiracy: Personal and Social Transformation in the 1980s.* Los Angeles: J.P. Tarcher, 1980. A broad look at the many ways in which people are currently working toward the "New Age" and the leaderless, but powerful, network that is evolving.

Hancock, Arthur B, and Kathleen J. Brugger. *The Game of God: Recovering Your True Identity.* St. Louis: Humans Anonymous Press, 1993. A light, yet very profound, exploration of the human condition, with cartoons on every page, laying out a universal 12-step program for the recovery of our true identity.

HARMAN, WILLIS. *Global Mind Change*. Indianapolis: Knowledge Systems, 1988. An excellent analysis of the basic crises facing humanity, arguing for an evolutionary transformation of society as the only viable means of resolving them in the long term. Well worth reading.

HOYLE, FRED, and N.C. WICKRAMSINGE. *Lifecould: The Origin of Life in the Universe*. New York: Harper & Row, 1979. The evidence for "panspermia", the theory that life originated in outer space.

HUXLEY, ALDOUS. *The Perennial Philosophy*. London: Fontana, 1958. A now-classic collection of passages from mystics, prophets, and saints who have approached direct knowledge of the Divine, bringing out the common themes that run across cultures and time.

JANTSCH, ERIC. *The Self-Organizing Universe*. Oxford and New York: Pergamon, 1980. An account of the whole evolutionary process from Big Bang to Gaia, from the perspective of dissipative systems, showing evolution as a natural consequence of physical laws. Also recommended as one of the most readable introductions to the theory of dissipative systems.

KING, ALEXANDER, and BERTRAND SCHNEIDER. *The First Global Revolution: A Report by the Council of the Club of Rome*. New York: Pantheon Books, 1991. A very thorough analysis of the global problematique and the shifts in thinking and values that need to occur, by two of the founding members of the Club of Rome.

KOPELMAN, ORION. *The Second Ten Commandments*. Palo
Alto: Global Brain, 1995. The ten commandments that we
should be following today if we are to live in harmony with
each other and our planet.

KUHN, THOMAS. *The Structure of Scientific Revolutions*. 2d
Ed. Chicago: The University of Chicago Press, 1970. The
original and definitive work on scientific paradigms and
paradigm shifts.

LASZLO, IRWIN. *The Inner Limits of Mankind: Heretical Reflections on Today's Values, Culture and Politics*. London:
Oneworld Publications, 1989. A remarkably clear exposé
of the problems of contemporary society and the urgent
need for fundamental reappraisal of man's treatment of his
planet, by one of the foremost exponents of systems theory.

LEONARD, GEORGE. *The Transformation: A Guide to the Inevitable Changes in Humankind*. Los Angeles: J.P. Tarcher, 1981.
A very readable overview of the changes in consciousness
and society from a human potential perspective. Also, *The
Silent Pulse* (New York: Dutton, 1978). Our identity and
our interconnectedness; how getting in touch with the underlying pulse can help personal transformation.

LOVELOCK, JAMES. *Gaia: A New Look at Life on Earth*. London
and New York: Oxford University Press, 1979; and *The Ages
of Gaia*, London and New York: Oxford University Press,
1988. The "Gaia Hypothesis" by one of its formulators.
Details the physical, chemical, and biological evidence for
the suggestion that the Earth is an organism in its own right.

LUX, KENNETH. *Adam Smith's Mistake: How a Moral Philosopher Invented Economics and Ended Morality.* Boston: Shambhala, 1990. A profoundly important book showing why "the invisible hand of self-interest" no longer works in today's world.

MILLER, JAMES GRIER. *Living Systems.* New York: McGraw-Hill, 1978. Miller's 1000-page magnum opus on the general theory of living systems, detailing how the nineteen critical subsystems of life can be found at all levels, from the single cell to supranational systems.

MURCHIE, GUY. *The Seven Mysteries of Life.* Boston: Houghton Mifflin, 1978. Seventeen years in the writing and worth every minute of it. A most imaginative and inspired look at life, from crystals to the whole planet, touching on just about everything and very simply explained. Highly recommended.

MYERS, NORMAN, ed. *The Gaia Atlas of Planet Management: For Today's Caretakers of Tomorrow's World.* London: Pan Books, 1985. Packed full of data, and with vivid graphics, this book spells out what we must do in order to better manage our environment. An important book for anyone concerned with the welfare of the planet.

POLAK, FRED. *The Images of the Future.* Translated by E. Boulding. San Francisco: Jossey-Bass, 1973. One of the principal books on the role of social images in shaping the future.

SAHTOURIS, ELISABET. *Gaia: The Human Journey from Chaos to Cosmos.* New York: Pocket Books, 1989. The evolution of life on earth, told from a Gaian perspective. An excellent survey of how we got here and the issues facing us today.

SHELDRAKE, RUPERT. *A New Science of Life: The Hypothesis of Formative Causation.* Los Angeles: J.P. Tarcher, 1982. A challenging book, suggesting that biological systems are regulated by invisible organizing blueprints (morphogenic fields). An ingenious explanation of the transference of behavior across large distances, which, if scientifically supported by further research, will challenge the current biological paradigm.

SIMONTON, CARL AND STEPHANIE. *Getting Well Again.* Los Angeles: J.P. Tarcher, 1978, and New York, Bantam, 1978. The role that visualization and meditation can play in the healing of cancer, although the principles apply to any illness.

SRI AUROBINDO. *The Life Divine.* Pondicherry, India: Sri Aurobindo Ashram, 1970. Sri Aurobindo's 1,000-page magnum opus, in which he carefully and logically lays out his basic philosophy on the evolution of man and his future ascent into "Supermind". It is, however, slow and exacting reading. A good readable introduction to Aurobindo's ideas is the selection of writings contained in *The Mind of Light* (New York: Dutton, 1971).

STACE, WALTER. *Mysticism and Philosophy.* London: MacMillan, 1960. A thorough and lucid analysis of the writings of mystics and religious teachers, emphasizing their common beliefs.

STAPLEDON, OLAF. *Star Maker.* London and New York: Penguin, 1972. One of the most far-reaching science fiction books ever written. More of an evolutionary projection than science fiction—from humanity to Gaia to the galaxy and beyond. A must. First published in 1937, it is only now becoming widely acclaimed.

TARG, RUSSELL, and HAROLD PUTHOFF. *Mind-Reach.* New York: Dell, 1978. Some of the most recent and convincing research into our latent powers of ESP.

TART, CHARLES. *Waking Up: Overcoming the Obstacles to Human Potential.* Shaftesbury: Element Books, 1988. Charles Tart has for many years been a leader in the field of altered states of consciousness, and in this book shows how we can overcome the cultural conditioning and habitual attitudes that have become barriers and limitations to our true consciousness.

TEILHARD DE CHARDIN, PIERRE. *The Phenomenon of Man.* New York: Harper and Row, 1965. Probably his best-known work, although it only presents a partial view of his ideas. Some people find it difficult reading. The best general introduction to his thoughts is *Let Me Explain,* edited by John-Pierre Demoulin (New York: Harper and Row, 1970), which, as well as being an excellent primer, will also direct the interested reader through Teilhard's many writings.

THOMPSON, WILLIAM IRWIN. *Passages About Earth.* New York: Harper and Row, 1973. Also his *Darkness and Scattered Light.* New York: Anchor/Doubleday, 1978. Two books by the visionary founder of the Lindisfarne Association exploring the possibilities for a planetary renaissance.

VAUGHAN, ALAN. *Incredible Coincidence.* New York: Lippincott, 1979. The first major collection of synchronicity case histories.

WATSON, LYALL. *Lifetide.* London: Hodder and Stoughton, 1979. The growing awareness that "we are all one" examined from a biological and evolutionary perspective, complete with an excellent and fascinating collection of supporting data.

WATTS, ALAN. *The Book: On the Taboo Against Knowing Who You Are.* New York: Random House, 1972. Watt's very readable book on the "skin-encapsulated ego".

WEINBERG, STEVEN. *The First Three Minutes: A Modern View of the Origin of the Universe.* New York: Basic Books, 1976. A clear exposition of current scientific opinion on what happened during the "Big Bang" and immediately afterwards.

WILBER, KEN. *The Atman Project.* Wheaton, Ill.: The Theosophical Publishing House, 1980. "The theme of this book is basically simple: development is evolution, evolution is transcendence, and transcendence has its final goal Atman, or ultimate Unity Consciousness. . . ." So begins Wilber's book. It's not light reading, but it is probably the most comprehensive investigation of inner evolution in print. A very important book.

ZUKAV, GARY. *The Seat of the Soul: An Inspiring Vision of Humanity's Spiritual Destiny.* London: Rider, 1990. Written from the heart, Gary Zukav explores the many ways we can change the way we live and relate to others, and put our spirituality into practice.

VIDEO: A video by the author based on the ideas in *The Global Brain Awakens* is available from the publishers. See order form at end of book.

INDEX

ORDER FORM: For further products by Peter Russell

QTY	TITLE	PRICE	TOTAL
☐	**THE GLOBAL BRAIN AWAKENS:** **Our Next Evolutionary Leap, Peter Russell**	$22.	_____
☐	**GLOBAL BRAIN VIDEO, Peter Russell** Awarded the Grand Prix and Gold Award by the Swedish Audio/Visual Festival and rated "4 stars" by the Video Rating Guide. The Global Brain Video presents what many leading edge thinkers feel are "Some of the most important ideas in the world at the moment." 35 Minutes.	$30.	_____
☐	**THE GLOBAL BRAIN AWAKENS AUDIO,** **Peter Russell** Two one hour tapes	$15.	_____
☐	**THE CREATIVE MANAGER,** **Peter Russell and Roger Evans** Heralded by John Sculley, former CEO and Chairman of Apple Computer, Inc., as "A sensational book on personal empowerment. The real revolution in the Information Age is the ability to use our minds differently. *The Creative Manager* will be your guide." Hardcover.	$26.	_____
☐	**THE WHITE HOLE IN TIME: Our Future Evolution** **and the Meaning of Now, Peter Russell** "Creates the sense of urgency that propels change." Michael Ray, author of *The New Paradigm in Business*. A revolutionary study of humanity's place in the universe. A book that raises questions, offers hope, and explores alternative possibilities to the destiny of humanity and Earth. Softcover.	$11.	_____
☐	**THE WHITE HOLE IN TIME VIDEO, Peter Russell** Shown at Stanford University's Business School classes. Integrating scientific understanding of the physical cosmos with the spiritual underpinnings of the human mind, *The White Hole in Time* challenges us to abandon our egocentric view of the world and awaken to our full potential. Music by Vangelis. 25 Minutes.	$30.	_____
☐	**THE BRAIN BOOK, Peter Russell** "Within our heads lies one of the most complex systems in the known universe." This handbook for brain users sets out the brain's structure and development; examines its functions and potential, discussing memory, imagery, mnemonics, the holographic theory of mind, reading and note-taking. Of special interest to anyone wishing to expand their appreciation of the brain, and a great help for improving reading and study skills. Softcover.	$10.	_____
☐	**THE TM TECHNIQUE, Peter Russell** Introduces Transcendental Meditation, its origins; how it works, producing a state of profound rest, exactly opposite to the accumulation of stress and tension; and its implications for health, clarity of mind and creativity. Also looks at the higher states of consciousness to which TM can lead; and considers the implication for society as a whole. Softcover.	$10.	_____

Shipping and handling: Book rate: $2.00 for first item, .75 for each additional item. Priority: $4.00, + $1.00 for each additional item.   _____ _____
California residents add 8.25% sales tax.   _____ _____
Green tax 5%, a *voluntary* contribution to be distributed by Global Brain™ to environmentally restorative projects.   _____

TOTAL _____

GLOBAL BRAIN INC.
MAIL TO: 555 Bryant Street # 210
            Palo Alto, California, USA, 94301-1703
FAX TO: 415/327-2028 or call 1-800-U-G0-GLOBAL
PAYMENT METHOD: Make check payable to Global Brain Inc.
Visa, American Express, Discover Card
Credit Card # _____ Exp. Date _____